AF380117

What Others Are Saying
About Ayako Kondo and This Book

"Ayako Kondo is like a lotus flower that blooms looking straight up. Perhaps for every pure tear that Ayako shed, her roots spread deeper and wider. Living with love can sometimes be challenging, but that's why encounters with people who embody it are precious. They inspire us to nurture our own flowers into bloom. A big mahalo for encountering Ayako! Cheers to *Embracing the Art of Love*! For those who want to see their own flowers, I recommend reading this book, which traces the journey of Ayako's heart."

—Yasuko Claerbout, Maui, Hawaii

"In this beautiful book, *Embracing the Art of Love*, Ayako Kondo offers a loving perspective for you to look at yourself and everything around you. As I read her book, I felt like Ayako was sitting across from me sharing her life stories, and I could feel her love—her genuine love for people, the world, the earth, and the universe. As you read, you will find yourself immersed in Ayako's journey, but also in your own journey to meet your true self. I hope everyone enjoys their journey in this safe and loving space that Ayako has created throughout this book."

—Yoriko Grimes, Club Tuesday Member

"In essence, Ayako Kondo is a soothing presence who effortlessly puts your heart at ease. This book offers a unique opportunity for readers to embark on a journey guided by Ayako, where they can discover the joy of exploring a beautiful world and bask in the warm embrace of her tranquil love. My hope is that numerous individuals will encounter and embrace this happiness, fostering a sense of well-being inspired by Ayako's gentle spirit."

— Yurika Lazo, Club Tuesday Member

"If you find yourself holding this book, congratulations are in order, for you may have just unlocked the enchanting world of 'the art of love.' Within these pages lies a captivating journey, a tapestry woven with threads of warmth, wisdom, and the transformative power of love."

— Kazuko Boeker, Founder of Body Wellness Hawaii

"Immersed in love, Ayako Kondo resembles the serene and embracing sea, making her departure from Maui truly startling. Yet, amid the surprise, the silver lining is the exquisite legacy she has left behind through her beautiful writing. Anticipating its eventual publication in Japanese, this heartfelt narrative holds the promise of reaching even more souls with its touching and profound message."

— Kazuko Nakajima, Founder of Mahinahina Maui

"Ayako is akin to a flower, effortlessly instilling a sense of beauty and relaxation in those around her, encouraging authenticity and kindness. This book serves as a portrayal of the divine feminine, articulated by someone embodying the essence of divine femininity in human form. If you seek answers and guidance on living a life centered on love, both giving and receiving, this book is a profound and invaluable resource for you. It unfolds the wisdom and grace of Ayako, providing a path to embrace and embody the transformative power of love in your own life."

— Naomi Leibow, Owner of Salon Crystal Cave

"Ayako radiates love in every interaction. Her kindness, support, and willingness to assist others have earned her the trust of those around her. Over the years, my own need for nurturing has been profoundly fulfilled through encounters and interactions with her. This book represents my aspiration for humanity—to share Ayako's wisdom through promoting love, compassion, and kindness on a global scale. It stands as a beacon, offering insights that can inspire positive change, fostering a world where the warmth of love and compassion flourishes."

— Yuko Takahashi, Founder of Something Great Hawaii

"This book transcends cultural, national, religious, political, age, and gender boundaries, making it a valuable read for everyone. Ayako's story and the wisdom embedded within these pages are universal, offering insights that resonate with individuals from all walks of life. It serves as an inspiring guide for those seeking empowerment, growth, and a deeper connection with the profound qualities of strength, humility, and the pursuit of knowledge."

— Fusayo Luksic, Lomilomi Massage Therapist, Maui, Hawaii

"Whether you are lonely, sad, discouraged, or moderately happy and want to know greater happiness, the answer is always love. In *Embracing the Art of Love*, Ayako Kondo reveals how you can learn to love yourself and others on a deeper level. She shares her personal story of growing up in Japan, living in Hawaii, losing her husband to cancer, and finding reminders of God's love all around her. Now she's here to help you also know greater love. Get ready to raise your vibration!"

— Patrick Snow, Publishing Coach and International Best-Selling Author of *Creating Your Own Destiny* and *The Affluent Entrepreneur*

"Ayako Kondo shares deep truths about human existence in this revolutionary book that teaches us how better to love, how to forgive, how to practice self-love, and how to embrace suffering in a way that allows us to see it as an adventure in learning. When you embrace the art of love, you will be embracing hope, change, and happiness for all of humanity and the world."

— Nicole Gabriel, Author of *Finding Your Inner Truth* and *Stepping into Your Becoming*

EMBRACING THE ART OF

Love

Healing Your Past
Regaining Your Power
Following Your Soul

AYAKO KONDO

AVIVA
PUBLISHING
New York

DEDICATION

To my son, Kei Hashimoto. I am so proud of the young man you have become. You are a brilliant, caring, and compassionate human. I am honored to have this lifetime opportunity to raise you as a mother, and it is my greatest fortune to have you as my son. You are my biggest motivation to make the world a better place. I thank you so much for existing. Whatever path you will take, it is meant to be, and I believe in you. Be kind to yourself, be passionate, and love fully. I love you.

To my parents, Tadashi and Toshiko Kondo. I am deeply grateful for both of you for raising me to become who I am now. I feel very fortunate for all of my challenging experiences because they were blessings that helped me break out of the invisible shell I was given since I was born to you. I know you love me, and I love you always.

To you, the reader, may this book allow you to enliven your inner love and then be so inspired that you spread your love throughout the world.

ACKNOWLEDGMENTS

I am grateful to the many people whose presence helped me create this book. I'd like to begin by expressing my sincere gratitude for Graham Simmons, my deceased husband, whose soul continuously encourages me to live as who I am and follow my dreams.

I'd like to thank my family and many of my friends for their encouragement and for contributing their insights to the process of creating this book, especially Haruki Ohta, Kaori Iwatake, Kazuko Boeker, Yasuko Claerbout, James Dharman Reed, and my divine feminine group of friends at Waiakoa Wildflowers in Maui.

My gratitude to my families and friends in California, whose presence was a huge support for me and who live in many of the beautiful parts of my memories.

To the people in Maui, I feel so fortunate to be a resident of this beautiful island. A devastating fire burned thousands of houses on the island on August 8, 2023, while I was in the middle of creating this book. People, including children, are still missing, water is contaminated, and losses are unmeasurable. My sincere prayers are with all the people on the island. You are always close to my heart.

To the ancestors and spirits in my native country of Japan who have supported me in getting where I am today. I thank you, and I am honored and proud to call Japan my motherland.

Special thanks to the people who contributed to the physical creation of this book: Patrick Snow, international best-selling author, professional keynote speaker, and publishing coach, who has been supporting me since the beginning in writing the book and who has helped to keep me inspired and has lifted the pressure when I felt stuck. He has been the biggest and most reliable cheerleader along the way. Kana Anan, designer of the beautiful cover image, whose artistic talent I admire. Nicole Gabriel at Angel Dog Productions for her adept interior design. Susan Friedman at Aviva Publishing for her experienced advice. Tyler Tichelaar and Larry Alexander at Superior Book Productions for their expert editing and advice.

CONTENTS

Awakening in Love

"Your task is not to seek for love, but merely to seek and find
all the barriers within yourself that you have built against it."

— Rumi

*Y*ou *are*, in your soul's essence, a being of love! You *are* the miracle child who was born from love, born with love, and exist as love! That is the principle of us humans on this planet earth, which is the planet of love.

We are living in a critical time in human and earth history. Many of us are called upon to contribute solutions to world, national, and local problems and crises, which can be done in many different ways based on our individual talents. Despite your wish for wellbeing for yourself and others, you may be struggling to maintain your serenity since our current world situation does not seem favorable. When you think of the economy, the environment, health, the hope for world peace, family life, and the future, none of them may seem bright or promising.

You may have realized your satisfaction in finding or achieving love cannot be attained without the capacity to love yourself, and you may have also realized how important courage and faith are in order to be loving and compassionate. This book will show you how to pursue the art of love. In *Embracing the Art of Love*, I wish to convey to you that no matter what your personality and interests, your essential core is love.

You may be wondering, "Why does greed, cruelty, conflict, poverty, misery, and endless suffering exist in the world?" or "Why are all my attempts for love bound to fail?" Do you remember when you first wondered what love is? Have you gotten any answers to your questioning the meaning of love from anybody, or have you found love? How do you feel about your life right now, whether or not it is filled with love?

I feel your pain and confusion. I have gone through divorce, separation by death of loved ones, and breakups. I have also put lots of energy and passion into my work and established a food business, an organic farm, and a sanctuary. I had these past experiences while living in different places and countries. Today, I have the ongoing challenge of aging parents. While overcoming many hurdles, I have been searching for love and answers to what love is, where it is, and how I can attain and spread it to the world. For many years, John Lennon's song "All You Need Is Love" has rung in my ears. If it's true that all we need is love, why does it seem so difficult for us to live with love, have peace of mind, and be compassionate with each other?

In this book, you will learn that the art of love starts within, and it is necessary for you to go inside yourself and find your authentic self to live the art of love. Your body is your sacred vessel that holds your mind and spirit. By maintaining your sacred vessel daily, you can grow toward great unity of mind and spirit.

The art of love starts by loving yourself; in order to give to yourself, you must be curious about what your inner callings are and be passionate about finding them. If your passion can be shared in a safe environment and be supported by a group of like-minded people, you will feel safe, comfortable, and more confident in pursuing your passion.

Your true self is often hidden beneath many layers of your parents/caregivers' values, patterns, and influences. You must work on healing your inner motherhood and fatherhood, and you must find a way to embrace your inner divine feminine regardless of whether you are male or female. By cultivating it, we can remember how good we are and realize how much love we carry within us and for others.

As soon as you start paying attention to what is going on in your heart, you will notice sometimes there are multiple layers. You may see only what you are capable of seeing at that time, so you need patience. Over time, you will learn to feel the pain, work through your grief, release your pain, heal, and love again.

Self-confidence is the number-one thing that helps you set yourself free from the chain of heaviness in difficult situations and regain your power to stand up. It is like the yang aspect of self-empowerment. On the other hand, self-love is something you also predominantly get by your own effort and willpower, but it is more yin, which you work on inwardly and give rather than gain from.

We are connected with other lives, the planet, and the Universe through our roots, and especially with people with whom we have close relationships and whom we can relate deeply to over lifetimes. All you need to do is feel, and to do that, do not be afraid to love. Life is short, yet our soul is eternal. Love brings you joy in living, so love fully.

By treating yourself as a whole, and realizing you have mysterious, yet extraordinary power to make miracles, you can live to your full potential and spread positive vibrations, not only to yourself but to other people, society, your country, the world, future generations, and the whole universe. If you focus on unconditional love, which you receive from your ancestors and the great spirits around you or from the Universe, you realize the importance of passing down love to your children and future generations. If you go deeper into your heart and remember where you came from, your soul knows that in order to transform the suffering into love, which can be done very simply, you must believe in the presence of a god/goddess, the Soul of the World, and that we are all connected as families in this universe.

You are on a hero/heroine's journey by living the art of love; it is a quest accomplished by healing your past, finding your purpose, and empowering your soul. I hope you use this book as your treasure map for those goals. If you apply the wisdom, knowledge, experience, skills, strategies, and techniques offered in this book to your life, you will find your own treasure of love in your life.

I am honored to share my knowledge and wisdom in this book. It is based on what I have learned through my experiences and from many great souls who have practiced the art of love before me. I was born and raised in Japan as a daughter in a traditional family where four generations lived under the same roof. I longed for freedom from an early age, but that seemed impossible to attain unless I changed my life in drastic ways. I moved to different places and countries, was in different relationships, changed careers, adopted spiritual practices, and studied different philosophies for mental and physical wellbeing. Through all these different experiences, encounters with different cultures and beliefs, and the knowledge I gained, I was led over and over to see the importance of love. Just as you opened this book in search of love, I am enjoying my quest for love every day and enjoying being a lifelong practitioner of the art of love.

A philosophy I live by is embodied in this quote I wrote many years ago:

"Imagine a world where all mothers are smiling.
Hold the warmth in your heart.
See the light your soul radiates.
You are the creation of love.
Love is who you are."

It is my greatest joy to walk the path of the art of love with you. We are all walking each other home, and to your soul, home is love. Are you ready to live the art of love? If so...good; let's get started and take this journey together!

Ayako Kondo

Chapter 1

Connecting to Your Soul

"Like a path frequently traveled becomes clear and well-marked in the forest, so too does the path to your Soul become more clearly marked in your consciousness."

— Genevieve Gerard

When you connect to your soul, you find your power spot. Your power spot is where you gain confidence and direction. As you start your journey on the path of the art of love, you may wonder where to begin. The path is within you, in your soul. In this first chapter, let's look at how to clear the path and maintain it so it becomes easier to connect with your soul. As you get used to going within, or if you naturally know how to connect to your soul no matter what circumstances you face, you may not need to go physically to the power spot, but it is easier if you have an actual spot that you bring your physical body to where you feel deeply at home and serene.

POWER SPOT FOR YOUR SOUL

Do you have a power spot? What is a power spot, and how do you define it?

A power spot is a place from which you get energy and power. It is where you feel peaceful, relaxed, and restful. When you get there, you remember who you are. You give your heart some tranquil time as you surround yourself with clean and gentle air. You feel clear in your head, and you reassure yourself you are safe. In your power spot, you regain your confidence by being yourself. That is your power spot.

A year after my husband Graham died from brain cancer, I was coping with grief while I was still living in the Bay Area of San Francisco, California. I spent nine years of our married life there before he passed away. Shortly after Graham's death, I flew to Maui, Hawaii, over a weekend, hoping to find a new place to live. Although I enjoyed my life in the Bay Area, my intuition was telling me it was time to move. It was my soul calling me to go wherever my heart desired. I am so glad I followed its calling.

In a rental listing for Maui, I found a property that interested me. When I first drove onto the property, I saw vivid green plants in different hues and bright red and magenta flowers all shining brightly as they reflected the sun's rays. A gentle breeze was caressing my hair and cheeks, and the view down the hill was of the sky-blue ocean. Everything was so beautiful that I felt like I was in a movie, and I had a deep sense of being welcomed here. I strongly felt, "Oh, I really want to live here. This is my home." That is how I decided to move to Maui and start my new life.

Interestingly, it was exactly one year after Graham's death.

Thinking back, I must have been feeling the land's healing energy. I felt the relaxing, gentle, and soothing energy of nature and the place, and it was exactly what I needed at the time. I was not aware then, but now, eight years later, I know how much pain I was still carrying from the loss of my loved one.

TOUCHING THE EARTH, LOOKING UP TO THE SKY

Gone with the Wind is my favorite movie. The story of the main character, Scarlett O'Hara, left such a powerful impression on me when I first watched the movie as a high school student in Japan. I got goose bumps when Scarlett went back to her once flourishing plantation, Tara, and found her home devastated by the Civil War. She knelt on the ground and dug into the earth for food, finding herself miserable, hungry, and exhausted. Then she looked up at the sky sobbing and pledged never to be hungry again.

I have never experienced physical hunger the way Scarlett did, but in my soul, I have known moments when I felt as broken as she did. What I did in those difficult moments was seek my own Tara, in my heart, where I could cry out and make a new pledge. When you face challenges and difficulties, if you touch the earth and look up at the sky from Tara, the place of your origin, which is always there in your heart whenever you need to return there, you will find your inner peace and the bright light of your own soul. That place gives you the energy to stand up again.

The key to returning to your Tara is to maintain the path to get there. Only you can take that path, just as Scarlett did when she figured out her way home by herself.

PATH TO YOUR POWER SPOT

Do you make daily time for yourself so you can have a quiet moment to feel relaxed and restful? If you have a corner for yourself at home, perhaps you may set up your sacred table—a place to sit still, close your eyes, and meditate. That place becomes your power spot. If it is hard to create your own corner in your home environment, you do not have to set it up. You can go to a nearby café, find a bookshelf at the library, or a gingko tree (or whichever trees you have) at the park. Your power spot can be anywhere. And you can have multiple places. The idea is to have a spot where you can take a deep breath and calm your mind.

A few years ago, I met a woman named Naomi who was visiting Maui. She was from a small island off the coast of Okinawa, Japan. It is a remote island where nature is preserved, and it has a tradition and culture of its own. Residents know each other there, and they never lock the doors of their houses because it is so safe and crime free. In 2016, despite the protest of residents, the government decided to build a US military base there because the island is close to the border with Taiwan. When I met Naomi on Maui, the US was about to start building the base. She came to visit Maui because she was disappointed and depressed, afraid her sacred island was going to change. It would no longer be the safe and peaceful paradise she had taken refuge in after twenty years of living in the big city of Tokyo.

One day, Naomi and I went for a hike in the forest on Maui at Waihee Ridge Trail. We enjoyed nature's scenery—we picked pink guava fruits from the tree along the trail, saw fuchsia-colored wild orchids blooming, watched the river running in the valley, heard waterfalls splashing over the cliffs, and enjoyed hearing a nightingale singing. We had a magnificent view of the ocean from the top of the hill, and we could see Molokai over the blue water. We sat and had a little snack, and we both felt so refreshed in the fresh air. We were comfortably tired physically, but we felt relaxed and rejuvenated.

On our way back along the trail, we stopped at a big tree. Naomi put both her arms around the tree trunk. She hugged the tree and started to cry. I was standing behind her, looking at her back shaking as she sobbed. I let her cry for a little while. Then I walked toward her and hugged her and the tree from behind. I felt her heartache, and at the same time, I felt the tree's energy streaming into our beings.

A few days later, when Naomi left Maui to return to her island, she told me she was thinking about giving up her life on her dream island. She was trying to figure out whether she was going to stay on the island with a military base there—she had come to Maui for some quiet time by herself to think. On Maui, something had shifted in her mind, and she was able to let go of whatever was bothering her. She was ready to go back. I remember Naomi's bright smile, which looked as pure as that of a little child who has just shaken off the tears after crying loud and hard.

Naomi found the tree, her power spot, at the hiking trail on Maui. There she was able to open her heart to talk to it and cry out her pain.

Sometimes, all you need is a good cry and cleansing tears—and a power spot is a safe place to do an inner cleanse. The important thing is to recognize when you need your mind and heart cleansed and to avoid piling up aches inside your soul. Visiting your power spot helps you recognize the discomfort you are carrying. You can think of your power spot as checking in with your doctor, but it's even better than that because it costs you nothing, and no side effects result from the remedy you take from the power spot.

When Naomi flew out of the Maui airport, she left with an awakening soul, peace in her heart, and a willingness to move forward with living in peace despite her circumstances. As we are all taking our individual hero's journey, let us realize each experience has meaning, and each one is so precious. The places we go and the people we encounter exist as the set and cast in our own movie, which is filled with surprise and wonder. Naomi and I met on the island of Maui and shared beautiful moments together, and after we each went back to our own journey called life, the memories continued to exist eternally in our souls.

TAKING YOUR HERO'S JOURNEY

When I say "hero," I mean both hero and heroine.

Here are five ways I connect to my soul in everyday life. I believe you, too, can be authentically you by doing so.

1. **Have time for yourself to be in silence:** You notice how busy your mind is once you stop talking and pay attention. It is normal to

have an active, working mind—you do not have to fight with it to quiet it down. Instead, just have an observing eye. If you find yourself being critical or judgmental and unable to calm your mind, remember to be kind to yourself. Keep in mind that your biggest enemy might be your own habitual critical thoughts.

2. **Go to your power spot where you feel safe and serene:** As a human, you remember the feelings of comfort in your DNA when you are in nature. It is natural for you and for anyone to feel relaxed and peaceful when surrounded by greens, earth, clean water, and fresh air in a place where many other living beings reside.

3. **Close your eyes and smell the air:** When you use your senses, your feelings start dominating rather than your thoughts. That is when the path to your soul opens. Think of the air coming through your nose as the wind that opens the gate leading you to the path to your soul.

4. **Listen to the wind and birds:** I have heard that hearing is the last sense to go when people pass away. The sounds of nature and everything else around you are not mere sounds—they are vibrations brought to you as songs by spirits. Those spirits—your Higher Self, God, angels, the Universe, your ancestors, or whatever you name them—are trying to contact you and send you messages all the time. You can hear their songs once you open your heart and listen to them.

5. **Feel your breath filling each cell of your body:** Did you know in most cases a human's last breath is an inhale? When my husband

Graham was passing, I was watching him; his breaths were getting shorter and faster. Finally, he took a long breath in and then stopped breathing. Then his heart stopped beating. I've also heard we breath out when we are born. Breathing in when our life ends and breathing out when it begins is fascinating to me. So every time I breathe in, I try to feel it reaching every part of my body and going into every cell. I feel its energy keeping me alive, making me alive, and instantly, I am filled with gratitude for my existence in this lifetime.

EXERCISE

1. What in nature resonates with you the most? For example, you might like oceans, mountains, rivers, lakes, forests, waterfalls, snow, flowers, trees, stars, or rocks.

    ____

    ____

    ____

    ____

2. Where in the world would you travel to if possible? Think of a place where you would feel peaceful and serene.

    ____

    ____

    ____

    ____

3. Imagine you are there. Sit, take a deep breath, and close your eyes in this place. Write down the feelings and thoughts you experience.

____

____

____

____

4. Now, open your eyes and see how different you feel compared to before the exercise. Write down what you notice about how you feel different after using your imagination to go to your power spot.

____

____

____

____

5. Plan a visit to your place of power where your soul is calling as soon as possible. Write down when and where you will go.

____

____

____

SUMMARY

Do you make it a habit to check in with your soul every day? When was the last time you heard your soul calling? If you have not developed a habitual way to connect to your soul, I highly recommend finding your power spot. The power spot helps you calm your mind and tune into the voice in your heart rather than in your mind. It helps you activate your feelings rather than focusing on thinking. You can bring yourself to your power spot and remember who you are by putting yourself in a serene and peaceful environment—nature is best. Once you find your power spot, you can imagine you are there even when you do not have time to go to the actual spot physically, and you can feel the same relaxed state and connect to your soul. Remember, connecting to your soul is the first step on the path to finding the art of love.

Chapter 2

Maintaining Your Body as the Kingdom of God

"Everything we touch in our daily lives,
including our body, is a miracle.
By putting the kingdom of God in the right place,
it shows us it is possible to live happily right here,
right now."

— Thich Nhat Hanh

In the last chapter, we talked about how finding your power spot is one of the easiest ways to connect with the path to your soul. Your soul is where you practice the art of love. If you bring yourself to your power spot, you will feel peaceful and be able to get in touch with your true self easier than when surrounded by an environment where you are constantly stimulated in various ways. The art of love starts within, and it is necessary to get back inside yourself to see who the authentic you is and begin to live the art of love.

In this chapter, let's talk about your physical body as the sacred vessel, the kingdom of God. Have you ever noticed how ingenious your body is? When you see a newborn baby, are you mesmerized by how tiny their body is? Look at their toes and fingernails; they are so tiny, yet there are ten of them and each of them is functioning beautifully. If you put your finger close to the baby's hand, they can hold it tightly.

Humans have organs, blood vessels, nerves, and muscles. Researchers have found there are more than 100 trillion cells in our bodies, and they are constantly working, carrying fuel to our bodily functions, expanding and contracting, taking in and out, shedding and regenerating.

You, as a living human, are a sentient being; your physical body gets to feel life's sensations. Your body tells you when you feel tired and heavy or warm and vigorous. When you develop some sort of discomfort in your body, it is a sign to give yourself some downtime to travel the path to your soul. That is why it is so important for your body to function well—to get your signal working. Your body is helping you notice when something needs looking at or to be taken care of.

I consider maintaining the body is a form of prayer. By developing sensitivity to your physical sensations, you listen to your inner voice and connect to your mind, soul, and spirit. It is important to remember to treat your body as if God exists within it and to give it your utmost respect and gratitude.

BREATHING LOVE IN AND LOVE OUT

You must have heard how important proper breathing is, and you may be practicing breathing exercises daily. We have many different types of breathing exercises to choose from. I have learned different breathing techniques from different teachers of meditation and yogis, and I practice them daily. Among those techniques, the one that has stood out the most for me is one I learned from a qigong teacher. First, exhale to breathe love out. Then inhale to breathe love in. I was told to give love first, and when your lungs are empty, you naturally take love in to fill them with oxygen. Give before you take. You need space for love to come in. When you keep breathing love out and love in slowly and deeply, your body remembers the basic principle of love, as does your mind.

TWO PILLARS OF YOUR BODY

I have heard in some cultures, including Japanese, traditionally people had the sense of having two pillars in their body. In Western culture, and even when I was growing up in modern Japan, we learned to focus on one core pillar at the center of our body. In contrast, some Native people from the Pacific Rim, including Japanese, Mongolian, Alaskan, Aztec, Incan, and Hawaiian, had a sense of two pillars supporting the body—one pillar along the right side of the chest and the right leg, and another pillar along the left side of the chest and the left leg. For example, this sense can be seen in archery. In Western culture, an archer stands with one core at the center while in *kyudo* (Japanese martial art of archery), an archer stands with two pillars to draw a bow.

In Japan, we celebrate *bon* in summer. We believe *bon* is the period in which the spirits of our ancestors come back to revisit the family. This custom is based in Buddhism and Confucianism. It has been celebrated since ancient times. We visit the family cemetery, wash tombstones, leave flowers and offerings, light candles and incense, and give prayers to our ancestors.

Bon dance is a Japanese folk line dance specifically for *bon*. During *bon*, people gather at an open space, put a stage in the center with *taiko* drums and players and singers, make a circle around the stage, and everyone, including children and elders, dances in a circle. We draw no distinction between dancers and audience—anyone can participate. It is a dance to greet the spirits of ancestors and celebrate lives, theirs and ours.

One summer, I visited Gujo, in Gifu prefecture, Japan. Gujo is a small town with a population of about 15,000. What's special about this town is its *bon* dance, called the *Gujo Odori* Festival. The festival lasts thirty-one nights from the middle of July to early September, and during four nights of *bon* in mid-August, dances continue all night. About 300,000 people come to this small town every summer for the *Gujo Odori* Festival.

Growing up in Japan, *bon* dance was part of the tradition I never fully participated in nor had much interest in. Like many others from my generation, I grew up thinking the *bon* dance was an old people's thing, and there was nothing exciting or cool about it. After I moved to Maui, I found the *bon* dance is a big annual event in the local community because Maui has a history of Japanese immigrants coming to work in the cane fields in the 1800s. Ever since, Japanese culture, including *bon* dance, has become part of the local lifestyle.

I attended several *bon* dances on Maui. It was so alive and fun, and I started to enjoy the enthusiasm and atmosphere in celebrating the lives of our ancestors. I do not have direct relatives who immigrated to Hawaii, but I can relate to their feelings, their dreams and struggles with living in a foreign country, where the language and cultures are totally different.

When my friends on Maui invited me to go to the *Gujo Odori* Festival, I had just read an article about *Gujo Odori* in the local newspaper. On August 15, 1945, Emperor Hirohito announced to the nation over the radio that the Japanese government had accepted the Potsdam Declaration and surrendered to end World War II. The whole nation was devastated by the announcement because most people falsely believed the government propaganda that the military had been defeating their opponents. People of *Gujo*, broken-hearted, slowly came out of their houses, gathered around in the center of the town, and danced *Gujo Odori*. When I read the story, I wondered how they had felt seventy-seven years earlier when they had danced. I wanted to attend the festival to see what kinds of spirits the festival conjured up among people.

It was raining while we were putting on our *yukata* (a type of summer kimono when it is too warm to wear silk kimono layers). We were joking that if it kept raining, we would dance in the hotel room. As we wished, the rain stopped when we finished. We also wore *geta* (sandals made of cedar). We went to the street where *Gujo Odori* would take place that night. Lanterns were lit around the stage, and people dressed in different color *yukata* were gathering. Groups of families, friends, couples, locals, visitors, young children, and elders were waiting for the taiko drummers, *shamisen* players, flute players, and singers to start playing music for the dance.

Soon the music started and people in the circle started to dance. I followed a local friend and imitated her movements as I danced in the circle. As we danced to several songs, more people joined the circle. I started to feel as if we were in a different dimension. I was dancing as me in August 2022, and everybody else around me was there at the same time, but it was as if everyone in the dance circle were in a different world.

I also noticed in some songs, we put the arm and leg on the same side of the body forward together. The movements were unlike those in daily life. For example, when we put the right arm forward, the left leg should move forward at the same time, but in certain songs of the *bon* dance, we were supposed to move the same arm and leg together. That meant we had two pillars movement in the dance. When moving opposite appendages forward together, we have one pillar at the center of our body. We feel some tension at the core, but when we move the same side of the body, arm and leg, we have two pillars at either side of our body and no tension at the core.

It is as if you have emptiness at the center of your body. By holding the emptiness, you create space for spirits to come in. While I was dancing in two pillars movements, I was inviting spirits by embracing emptiness between the two pillars. I think that was partially why I had the mysterious feeling of being in a different dimension, and the feeling was full of delight and happiness. Perhaps I was dancing with spirits of ancestors who were visiting during *bon*, and we spent a wonderful time in the circle with other people and their ancestors. I kept on dancing until around 2 a.m., and I was not worn-out. Instead, I just felt a satisfied tiredness, as if I were a child again who played all day without a sense of time.

DAILY MAINTENANCE AND IMPROVEMENT

Here I want to share five activities I do every day to maintain my body and remain well rested and nourished. You can use these same activities or find your own ways that suit your body's needs, depending on your condition.

1. **When you wake up, drink a cup of warm water on an empty stomach:** I believe feeling warmth in the body is important to keep your energy flowing. Many articles have been written about how drinking a cup of warm water on an empty stomach balances the lymphatic system, regulates blood flow, and helps release toxins.

2. **Step into the backyard, do a simple qigong exercise, and alternate nose breathing:** It will not take long to start feeling better. Get fresh air, stretch your body, and breathe deeply—you will feel your energy start circulating and have more vitality.

3. **Get acupuncture treatment or bodywork before you are worn-out:** I noticed many people feel somehow guilty spending money for something intangible. You, as a seeker of the art of love, know the true value. Investing in feeling better is worth it because your physical and mental health are essential for growth and improvement.

4. **Watch your digestion and adjust according to your body's needs:** Studies show there are links between digestion, mood, health, and the way you think. Gut feelings, which result from intuition, have a connection to your brain, and together, they give you signals to continuously help in decision making. Thus, it is necessary to have a well-functioning gut by ensuring a good digestive system.

5. **Every night before going to sleep, ask yourself what your wishes are:** Think of things that make you happy. Be mindful to avoid thinking of things you feel you are lacking. Rather, make your wish as you do when you blow out the candles on your birthday cake or when you see a shooting star. Remember, angels can hear your wishes but not in negative form. While sleeping, your soul can leave your body partially and give your body full rest while it is traveling to different dimensions. By sending your soul off with your happy thoughts while you sleep, it can help you do things you do not know how to do.

EXERCISE

1. Feel the warmth in your stomach and visualize a radiant beam shining out of the spot in your stomach where you feel the warmth. What color is the beam of light? Use colored pencils to draw the light.

2. When you do nose breathing, try to focus on the area of your third eye and feel as if it is the top of a pyramid and the nostrils are the base. Write down your thoughts when you breathe in and out through your pyramid.

____

____

____

____

____

3. When was the last time you got a bodywork treatment? You can use a massage chair or other kinds of devices if you do not like to be touched. Set up a time and place and record it below.

____

____

4. What is your diet like? Are you comfortable with what you have been eating? Are you watching your digestion every day? If you have digestive issues, write down what you think is causing them.

____

____

____

____

____

____

____

5. Write down three wishes. One is something that can be easily achieved; another is one that you may need a miracle to make happen, and the third is something in between—not so easy, but not too difficult to achieve.

____

____

____

____

____

SUMMARY

Are you treating your body with enough respect and giving it tender care every day? Do you have vital energy filling your body, or do you feel tired and heavy? Remember to be sensitive to your bodily sensations and do not neglect its signals—because those signals are not only from your soul but also from spirit, including your guardian angels, ancestors, the Universe, nature, or God, whatever you call Spirit. Your body is your sacred vessel holding your mind and your spirit. By maintaining your sacred vessel daily, you can grow in great unity of mind and spirit. You are experiencing this lifetime with your body as a human being, which is still a spiritual being. Because you have your bodily sensations, you can resolve things that Spirit cannot by itself. By using your physical senses together with your mind and spirit, you embrace your whole self with gratitude for your life, and you can achieve greater love.

Chapter 3

Cultivating Intuition Through Your Five Senses

"Intuition is the key to everything,
in painting, filmmaking, business—everything.
I think you could have an intellectual ability,
but if you can sharpen your intuition,
which they say is emotion and intellect joining together,
then a knowingness occurs."

— David Lynch

Having a healthy body is fundamental to maintaining a good connection between your soul and the spirits around you and within you. As you read in the previous chapter, we are spiritual beings, and our body is where our spirits reside.

In this chapter, let's talk about intuition. Some people say intuition is your gut feelings, and if you cultivate your intuition, it becomes the feeling of knowing. As I mentioned in the last chapter, if you maintain healthy digestion, you get insight from within, which is your intuition. However, how do you know if your intuition is correct?

WHAT IS YOUR DESIRE?

Do you crave something sweet when you are tired or stressed out? I used to often, and I still have those moments occasionally, but not as often as before. Studies show when you are stressed, the brain requires more energy, about 12 percent more than normal. Carbohydrates provide the quickest energy, and something sweet gives you instant comfort because sweetness is the first taste you develop as a baby.

German anthroposophist Rudolph Steiner wrote in his book *An Outline of Esoteric Science*:

> In the spiritual world, no gratification exists for desires not already inhabited by the spirit in the sense-perceptible world. When death occurs, the possibility of satisfying these desires is cut off. The desire to enjoy good-tasting food can only be satisfied when the physical organs used in taking food are present—the palate, the tongue, and so on. After shedding the physical body, we no longer have these, and if the I still needs to have these desires satisfied, this need must remain unmet.

Steiner is pointing out that your spirit remembers your physical desires even after death. Your body goes back to the earth, but your spirit remains, and if you do not satisfy desires through taste or other physical comfort, they remain as if you feel raging thirst when there is no water. You carry that thirst in your spirit even after your body is gone.

Furthermore, Steiner said:

> To the extent that this desire is in accord with the spirit, it is present only as long as the physical organs are there, but to the extent that the I has created it without serving the spirit, it persists after death as a desire that yearns in vain for satisfaction.

My interpretation of this is if your physical desire is not satisfied through spiritual satisfaction, the desire remains after death as a deep longing.

How can we solve the issue of carrying the burden of unsatisfied desire even after death and into the next lifetime? Let's think about; if you crave chocolate, what feelings are behind the cravings? Do you crave the chocolate's bittersweet taste, rich velvety texture, and fragrance? Or do you crave the comfort you get by eating chocolate? If that is the case, think about why you need comfort in the moment. What is the true desire you are trying to satisfy by eating chocolate?

I had an eating disorder when going through a difficult time in my first marriage. I was frustrated and feeling lonely because I was misunderstood or got no empathy for what I was going through from my spouse. I felt like I was missing something. To compensate for what felt lacking in my heart, I filled my mouth with sweets—the quick comfort I could sense bodily.

I had the symptoms for years, but several years later, as I worked on spirituality and practiced different ways to gain confidence, one day I realized I no longer had the urge to eat a lot of sweets. I think that was because I had learned to understand my own needs and desires so I no longer depended on getting them met by others or by something else. Now, if I feel something is missing, I know it's important to focus on identifying what's missing and find a way to fulfill my true desire instead of compensating with something else that gives temporary relief.

ARTIFICIAL INTELLIGENCE (AI)

Artificial Intelligence (AI) is computer technology that allows us to build machines that mimic the human mind's capabilities. As technology continues to improve AI's abilities, AI can see things, hear sounds, smell fragrances, tastes foods, and touch things to distinguish objects. But can AI understand and create something new from information received using these five senses?

My friend Steve is a videographer. He did an interview with a ninety-year-old woman who is a local living on one of the minor Hawaiian islands. The interview was for a film Steve was producing for a client, and the client wanted him to record footage of their family business, which started on the island. The client was Caucasian, and their success relied on the local Hawaiian woman's support from the beginning.

While filming the interview, Steve was touched by the Hawaiian woman's story. He got emotional; his eyes got teary, and his nose got watery. Steve is not an emotional person, and he is very professional, keeping his mind calm and sharp, especially while he is working. However, it was one of those rare interviews where he was moved and did not suppress his emotions. When the woman noticed Steve was crying, she opened her heart even more, telling him exceptional stories. The emotional connection and communication between interviewer and interviewee helped make the film exceptional.

What if the interview had been conducted by AI? The most developed AI might have been able to read emotions using five senses. AI may have been able to see her body language and facial expression, to hear the tone of her voice over birds chirping in the background, to smell the fragrance of flowers in the air, and to feel the coolness of the glass of lemonade made with lemons from the tree in her yard. The AI might even have had knowledge of Hawaiian culture and Hawaii's history of being annexed by the United States. But could AI feel the emotions in the moment and respond with the strong emotions Steve felt that led to an outstanding interview?

Our power as humans lies in our unlimited creativity. Our five senses are directly connected to our emotions. Creativity is evoked by passion—a positive emotion that is strong, soft, sensitive, flexible, flowing, and communicative; thus, it amplifies and transmutes to the area where it taps into the limits of one's imagination. This positive emotion is called love. Creativity is the child of love.

INTELLECT GIVES MEANING TO EMOTION

Webster's Dictionary defines intellect as "the power of knowing as distinguished from the power to feel and to will: the capacity for knowledge." Intellect is the tool we use to recognize our emotions. Say we have an aha moment—a moment of sudden realization or discovery—and it comes from our intellect.

Helen Keller's famous story of how as a child she came to understand the word "water" is a wonderful example of how intellect brings light to emotion by giving it words and meaning. Below is an excerpt from Keller's autobiography, *The Story of My Life*.

> One day, while I was playing with my new doll, Miss Sullivan put my big rag doll into my lap also, spelled "d-o-l-l" and tried to make me understand that "d-o-l-l" applied to both. Earlier in the day we had had a tussle over the words "m-u-g" and "w-a-t-e-r." Miss Sullivan had tried to impress it upon me that "m-u-g" is mug and that "w-a-t-e-r" is water, but I persisted in confounding the two.

In this description, Keller reveals she did not understand the connection between objects and words. She was not yet able to understand each thing had a name.

> In despair she had dropped the subject for the time, only to renew it at the first opportunity. I became impatient at her repeated attempts and, seizing the new doll, I dashed it upon the floor. I was keenly delighted when I felt the fragments of the broken doll at my feet. Neither sorrow nor regret followed my passionate outburst. I had not loved the doll. In the still, dark world in which I lived there was no strong sentiment or tenderness.

Keller had no sentiment toward the object, which did not have meaning because she did not understand the concept of a name. All she felt in the moment was frustration in not being able to describe her emotion in words because she did not understand how to use the tool we call words to express thoughts and feelings.

> I felt my teacher sweep the fragments to one side of the hearth, and I had a sense of satisfaction that the cause of my discomfort was removed. She brought me my hat, and I knew I was going out into the warm sunshine. This thought, if a wordless sensation may be called a thought, made me hop and skip with pleasure.

Here Keller was relieved at being separated from the object, which she had broken out of frustration, and going outside to feel the warm sun. Maybe deep down, she felt some guilt, so she was glad to be given the opportunity to get away from the source.

> We walked down the path to the well-house, attracted by the fragrance of the honeysuckle with which it was covered. Some one was drawing water and my teacher placed my hand under the spout. As the cool stream gushed over one hand she spelled into the other the word water, first slowly, then rapidly.

This is a famous scene you may have seen in a movie or read in a book. The water scene shows Keller's great awakening as if she were being born into a new world of richness based on language and meaning.

I stood still; my whole attention fixed upon the motions of her fingers. Suddenly I felt a misty consciousness as of something forgotten—a thrill of returning thought; and somehow the mystery of language was revealed to me. I knew then that "w-a-t-e-r" meant the wonderful cool something that was flowing over my hand. That living word awakened my soul, gave it light, hope, joy, set it free! There were barriers still, it is true, but barriers that could in time be swept away.

The moment Keller made the first connection between the wonderful cool thing flowing over her hand and the word water, her soul was awakened as she realized the thing has its own living word.

I left the well-house eager to learn. Everything had a name, and each name gave birth to a new thought. As we returned to the house every object which I touched seemed to quiver with life. That was because I saw everything with the strange, new sight that had come to me.

This scene describes the joy of Keller's awakening. Everything she touched now had life, which gave her a completely new perspective on her world.

On entering the door I remembered the doll I had broken. I felt my way to the hearth and picked up the pieces. I tried vainly to put them together. Then my eyes filled with tears; for I realized what I had done, and for the first time I felt repentance and sorrow.

Moments earlier, Keller had broken the doll out of frustration with no sympathy, and now she felt sorrow as she realized what she had done for the first time. She realized she had broken the doll, and she was sorry because she discovered the doll had meaning.

> I learned a great many new words that day. I do not remember what they all were; but I do know that mother, father, sister, teacher were among them—words that were to make the world blossom for me, "like Aaron's rod, with flowers."

> It would have been difficult to find a happier child than I was as I lay in my crib at the close of that eventful day and lived over the joys it had brought me, and for the first time longed for a new day to come.

When Keller put together "the wonderful cool something" flowing over her hand and the word w-a-t-e-r written on her other hand, she had a sudden realization that brought her great joy. She suddenly started to see life in everything, and for the first time, she felt sorrow for the doll she had broken.

OBSERVE SENSATIONS THROUGH YOUR FIVE SENSES

You live your everyday life rarely realizing how much you use your sentient abilities to distinguish things and situations and make decisions. But you realize how much you depend on scent when your nose is congested and can't smell things—you realize how uncomfortable it is to live without judging and discriminating via scent. You rely on scent to know if food is fresh or rotten.

We use our sentient abilities without recognizing how much we rely on them. Below, I have listed five things I enjoy daily through my five senses. These five things help me observe sensations through the five senses. Observation is the first step in realization, and once we realize, we can accelerate the process of getting in touch with our intuition.

1. **Pet your cat:** If you have a pet, touch your animal friend as often as you can, and take as much time as you can. If you have a cat, for example, you most likely love it dearly and enjoy petting it. When you stroke its soft, smooth hair and feel its round hip and warmth, you get a good sensation through your hand. Touching your cat brings you the joy of loving.

2. **Observe plants and their colors:** Go for a walk and look at plants. You will notice different hues of greens and the colors of flowers. We can see so many varieties of plants with so many colors in nature. Some plants look different depending on the weather or time of day, either under full sunshine, with a few raindrops, or under the moonlight. They give you the sense of relaxation and awe at the beauty in nature, which reminds you how grateful you are to live on earth.

3. **Enjoy the sound of chimes:** Get some chimes—I personally like bamboo chimes—and hang them at the entrance of your home. Ring them every morning. The gentle sounds of chimes make you feel calm and like you are in resonance with nature and its natural rhythm.

4. **Burn incense or light a candle:** Incense can be a powerful and handy tool to set the mood of a space. Light a candle and burn incense when you want to focus on something. The smell of incense helps you clear your mind and concentrate.

5. **Eat slowly and mindfully to better enjoy your food:** This one is also a reminder to myself. If you are like me, you may find yourself eating in a hurry, mindlessly, especially when you are in the middle of doing something or when your mind is occupied by other thoughts. When you enjoy each bite, feel the texture, and taste the flavor of the food, you get a sense of satisfaction, and you digest food so much better.

EXERCISE

1. What is your favorite memory with food? How old were you when you ate that food, who were you with, and how did you feel? Why do you think it became a fond memory?

____

____

____

____

____

____

2. Imagine what color makes you feel most secure and restful in your bedroom and set that color as the aura in the room before you go to sleep. In the morning when you wake up, write down how you feel after sleeping in the color.

____

____

____

____

____

____

3. Go outside and listen to the sound of nature. You may hear birds, raindrops, wind, leaves, etc. Use your imagination as if you are a child again. Have a conversation with nature and listen to what it is telling you. What is Mother Nature telling you now?

____

____

____

____

____

____

4. Get a rose blossom or petal. Rose is known as the flower with the highest vibration. Smell it and inhale the fragrance into your brain. Take a piece of paper and colored pencils and draw the rose. After drawing the rose, describe how you feel.

____

____

____

____

5. When you are in the kitchen cooking vegetables, touch and smell each of them. When breaking them into small pieces, if possible, use your fingers instead of a knife. Have a conversation with the vegetable. When you eat the dish, taste each bite of vegetables and observe how you feel. Write down any thoughts that come up.

____

____

____

____

SUMMARY

Insight and inspiration come from intuition, and insight and inspiration are the source of your creativity. Because you are a spiritual being with a body, which you, as a human being, are blessed with to feel bodily sensations, you are meant to develop the ability to tap into intuition by using your five senses. When you feel something through your body, take your time and observe the feelings you get. You will develop your intellectual ability to understand what your mind experiences. By cultivating both your senses and intellect, you can access your intuition more easily, more often, and more accurately.

Chapter 4

Keeping Passion Burning in Your Heart

"I have no special talents.
I am only passionately curious."

— Albert Einstein

In the previous chapter, you learned that intuition is the key to your creativity. You can develop intuition by using your five senses and observation skills and cultivate both insight and inspiration. In this chapter, let's talk about another factor, passion, which is essential for creativity.

CURIOSITY

Someone said curiosity will conquer fear even more than bravery will. I think that is true. If you think about times you made major decisions, including marriage, divorce, moving, getting a new job, and starting a new relationship, it must have started with curiosity. You were curious about something or someone, and you were passionate about finding out more and exploring more about it. That was where you got the power to make your own decision.

The famous children's book *Curious George* was written and illustrated by a German Jewish couple, Margaret Rey and H. A. Rey, and published in 1941. The late 1930s and early 1940s was a disruptive time in Europe, and the Nazis were poised to take control of Paris, where the couple lived and wrote the *Curious George* stories. Knowing the dangerous Nazis were approaching, they decided to escape Paris. H. A. made two bicycles out of spare parts, and early in the morning of June 14, 1940, the couple rode their bikes out of Paris. They brought little with them—warm coats and some food. They also brought five manuscripts, one of which was *Curious George*.

The Germans entered Paris just hours later, but the couple was already on their way to the French-Spanish border, where they sold their bicycles for train fare to Lisbon. From there, they fled to Brazil, then to New York City to begin their new lives as children's book authors.

Curious George, the timeless children's story about George, a cute and curious monkey, was saved by the passion of the two young artists. What if they had stayed in Paris out of fear of the unknown journey to unfamiliar places instead of fleeing and seeking a life in new lands? If they chose something more practical to bring with them for survival, such as clothes or more food, the manuscript would have been abandoned and may have never been published. I do not mean you should prioritize the impractical over practical things. I simply mean the true value of something cannot be measured by its material value. Because the Reys prioritized their creation, which was born and saved by their passion, the story of *Curious George* is loved by many children and adults to this day.

IS IT PURE?

Japan has a project called ONEART (oneart.jp). ONEART started with a mission to bring out passion in children with disabilities. In this program, various artists collaborate with children with disabilities to create art together. Each piece is different depending on the child's unique feelings and imagination. The artist gets inspiration from the child's original creation and contributes their talent and techniques to complete the piece of art.

The art is exhibited in various places and then sold. When the art is sold, 60 percent of the profit is used as a scholarship for the child who originally created the piece. When I looked at their paintings online, I found even the titles are fun: *Colorful Monster, Star Child, Mermaid's Love, World of Frog, Sea God,* and so on.

The art is a great example of the creativity within the children's inner world, their passion and curious minds. Collaboration with the artists' enthusiasm, which is stimulated by their own passion and curiosity, helps bring the children's creativity to life using the artists' talents and skills. You see beauty in the art because you can feel the pure joy and passion of both the artists and children.

JOY OF GIVING

It is surely a wonderful feeling to receive gifts of caring, time, and/or effort from others. But you find yourself equally, if not more, delighted when you give to others.

My friend Ken works as a salesperson at a startup company that advises homeowners about home renovations and helps them find the right contractors depending on their needs. Ken's job is to call potential clients and explain what the company can do to help them. If the client signs a contract with the company, Ken gets points. Points are used to calculate the sales team's pay.

Ken did not have much experience in sales when he started the job, so he struggled to get points, which kept his salary low. When I talked to him, he was full of doubt about his ability because he was unable to make sales. He was working hard, but he was not getting a good response from his potential clients, so he lost confidence. I told him not to take it personally; he was still very young, this job was merely a part of his journey, and it was his chance to learn something new, so he should not lose confidence.

A couple of months later when I talked to Ken, his voice was light and cheerful as he told me he was doing much better at his job. When I asked what had happened, he said, "I shifted my mind from focusing on getting points from the clients. Instead, I think about how I am giving them a service and helping them find the right contractors so they can be happy about their home renovation."

I was happy for Ken, and I was proud of him for finding his joy in giving and moving forward in his life's journey.

PASSION FOR YOURSELF

If you keep passion's fire burning in your heart, you soon realize the fuel you need for the fire is curiosity for yourself. Your keen interest in going deeper and deeper inside to find the truth about who you are and what you want to do is, indeed, an essential asset for your creativity.

In Japan, I once took a weaving class at my great-grandmother's birthplace, which is a fabric factory. (My great-grandmother's father was a wool manufacturer. I'll tell you more about her in Chapter 6.) Using organic cotton thread spun at the factory, I chose the colors and the pattern, followed the teacher's guidance about weaving, and made a scarf. From the various materials, thread, colors, and patterns, I chose white, light blue, and yellow organic cotton. I weaved in an *aya-ori* pattern, which is also my name written in the same *kanji* character.

As I was weaving, I became engrossed and lost track of time. The touch of thread changed into the texture of fabric, colors were put together and became a combination of flowing yellow, blue, and white, and patterns started to appear as I weaved. The weaving was accompanied by the rhythmic sound of the hand-weaving machine.

I felt like I was putting myself together, gathering different pieces of information hidden deep inside of me. I tapped into my interests and longing to connect to my ancestry, my eagerness to use naturally grown and processed materials, my taste for colors, and my desire to express something resembling my name and its meaning, and I put them all into the scarf. I love the product that resulted. It always brings back the fond memory of being immersed in the pure joy of creation, driven by my passion to connect to myself.

The great thing about art is it reveals something inside the creator. You can use different mediums to explore and create your own art depending on your curiosity. Everyone is an artist. You can't make a mistake or fail, and while you are making your art, it is purely playtime.

FOLLOWING PASSION LEADS TO THE ART OF LOVE

The art of love starts with loving yourself. To give to yourself, you must be curious about what your inner callings are for and be passionate about finding them. Below are five things you can do to keep a fire burning in the hearth of your heart.

1. **Immerse yourself in beauty:** Make a commitment to yourself to make everything in your life more beautiful. Go to music concerts or art exhibits. Let loose your imagination and explore the world of music, painting, or sculpture. You do not need a reason to like a specific piece of music or art. The field of your subconscious is much richer than what you can explain in words. Language merely describes what you see on the surface of your deep inner world. Focus your feelings on beauty and be in the moment.

    If you have ever been to a Japanese tea ceremony, you would have noticed that it elevates paying attention to beauty to an art. The host carefully chooses a bowl to serve tea, a sweet with seasonal ingredients, fresh flowers, a vase that matches the theme of the ceremony, and a painting with meaning to generate conversation among the guests. Every guest is expected to admire each of those settings. It is refined and highly detailed. You are supposed to have a humble attitude to show your gratitude to the host and to the beauty itself. By doing so, you make yourself tranquil and your sensitivity shines. Sensitivity helps you realize your passion, the fire burning in your heart. It can be attained when your mind is serene.

2. **Invest time in curiosity:** When you are curious about something, including information, places, and people, then spend time—your most precious asset—finding out more about the matter. You may find something beneficial, and more importantly, while investing time, you will most likely get excited learning about the thing, and that matters most of all. Happiness attained in the moment by fulfilling your curiosity lasts for a long time. It creates a different feeling than you might get from buying something, which lasts only a short time. Plan your investment of time.

3. **Attend art workshops and classes:** Make time to play. If, like me, you did not get a good grade in art at school, you may never have had an enjoyable experience with creating art. I always thought I could not paint, but I love colors. You may think you are not capable or not good enough to create art, but have you really tried? The perception you have of yourself and your ability may be just a judgmental view from some authority figure when you were young. Please remember, in art, there is no right or wrong. With a

little help from some skilled professional artist or teacher, you can play with your creative ideas and be an artist. The most important thing is to feel free and have fun.

4. **Carry your notebook or sketchbook:** It is good to capture your ideas and inspirations in the moment. Keep a notebook and a pen at your bedside, and when you wake up, write or draw the first thing that comes to mind. Keep your notebook in your purse or pack, and make a habit of writing or drawing whenever you feel inspired or feel something. Think of your notebook as your treasure box, which is connected to your inner world. It shows how rich you and your inner self are.

5. **Observe and listen to nature:** Nature is filled with the beauty of its colors, shapes, light reflections, textures, and sounds. Many objects, including flowers, trees, leaves, stones, insects, animals, humans, earth, water, sky, and stars abound in nature. Take your time and observe the details. You will notice how different they look every day and every second, depending on the weather, time, and their feelings and conditions. Each time is a new encounter with them, with God's miraculous creatures and the miracles of life.

EXERCISE

1. Listen to music or look at art you like. You may do so with someone in your family, friends, or others. Beauty can be appreciated even more, just like a good meal, with other people. Write down how you like the music or the art. List your favorite artists and musicians.

---

2. When was the last time you went to the bookstore or library and spent some time there? If you go there, take your time and browse through different books. What book did you pick up and flip through? What topic drew your attention? Was it fiction or nonfiction, on the topic of travel or architecture, a cookbook, or something else? This exercise shows what you are most interested in and what inspiration you want.

---

3. Browse through an event page to find a class that looks interesting. It may be a class in painting, cooking, jewelry making, flower arranging, or some other item you want to learn how to make. You may want to focus on the class to create something. If you feel intimidated about attending by yourself, ask a friend or family member to attend with you. Write down which class you decided to take.

____

____

____

____

4. Write down key words about what you are interested in. You may write a certain color, the name of a person, a particular place, some historical event, a religion, etc. It will help you identify what you want to know more about.

____

____

____

____

____

____

5. Take a piece of paper and draw a mind map. A mind map is an excellent tool for organizing your ideas and seeing an overview of your thoughts. Below is an example of a mind map. You can use different color pencils, and you can use multiple sheets of paper to develop the map as well.

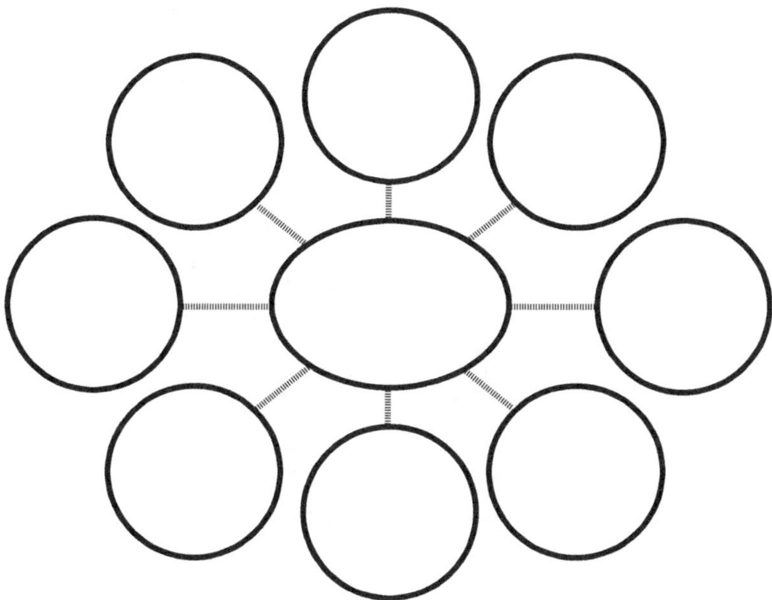

SUMMARY

Passion is the life source, and it guides you on the path of the art of love. By focusing on what you are passionate about, you maintain positive feelings toward something and toward your life as it naturally fulfills your heart's desire. Everyone is equally free in the world of one's passion because to follow passion, you must be curious about what's in your mind, and your mind is an asset no one should be allowed to take away.

Chapter 5

Cherishing Sisterhood/ Brotherhood

"Out beyond ideas of wrongdoing and right doing,
there is a field.
I'll meet you there."

— Rumi

Rumi's quote speaks to letting go of grudges. What I love about the above quote is that Rumi is asking us to look past others' imperfections and just love all people unconditionally. One way to do that is to spend more time with people, cherishing their presence.

In the previous chapter, you read how essentially important it is in the art of love to have passion to live. If your passion can be shared in a safe environment and supported by a group of like-minded people, you would feel safe, comfortable, and more confident in pursuing your passion. In this chapter, let's look at sisterhood/brotherhood, an area in which you can support and help each other grow.

USE YOUR HANDS

Waiakoa Wildflowers is a beautiful flower farm on the slope of Mt. Haleakala on Maui. Seasonal flowers, including rose, lily, dahlia, and poppy, and herbs are grown. The farm uses biodynamic farming methods, which originated before the organic farming movement and are holistic, ecological, and ethical. The flower farm is run by two young sisters and a group of volunteers called Club Tuesday, which started with a small group of only a handful of women. Members are invited to join the club, and each member feels honored to be invited to go inside and work at "the secret garden."

Every Tuesday morning, volunteers meet at a drugstore parking lot nearby and carpool to the site. I am a club member and very much enjoy the work. When we get to the farm, we are greeted by big smiles from the sisters and their mother, and their dogs are happy to see us. The family has a new member, Althea, who was born at the flower farm to one of the sisters in the spring of 2023. As of this writing, she still has not had her first birthday, and we are greatly amazed to see how much she grows every week and how much joy she brings to all of us. Most of the time, the work is focused on weeding around the flowers. It is simple hand work, yet I always feel better afterward. Something in the work of kneeling down on the ground, touching the earth, smelling the soil and plants, feeling the sunshine and breeze, hearing honeybees and birds, and being surrounded by flowers, butterflies, and trillions of microorganisms invisible to the eyes brings great joy. In addition to the beautiful environment, we work as a team, and while our hands are occupied with pulling weeds, we chat.

The club members are all Japanese women of different ages. We talk about life, such as parents, partners, children, jobs, the past, the future, the current situation, food, health, and all sorts of things. Some club members are more talkative than others, and some are good listeners. We work as we talk, and after about two-and-a-half hours, we look at piles of weeds we pulled out from the ground and smile at each other with great satisfaction and feelings of accomplishment. Spontaneously, someone will say, "I am hungry!" And it is lunchtime.

Potluck lunch at the table under the bamboo hut is like a picnic in the flower garden. The slight difference is we all contribute to the beauty of the scenery around us, including the food on the table and the maintained flowerbeds. We each prepare a dish to share, mostly Japanese food such as *onigiri* (rice balls), *tamagoyaki* (a rolled omelet), or *nukazuke* (fermented pickles). We are all hungry and comfortably tired after a couple of hours of farm work, and the food tastes especially delicious. We are in a cheerful and joyful mood and feel grateful to sit at the table with club members who come from different backgrounds and different life situations with different thoughts. No matter how different our lives outside the flower garden, during these few hours every Tuesday, we share the same feelings of appreciation for the land, beautiful flowers, and each other, like we are sisters.

In the old days when people were living in small villages, I am certain they had similar bonds. Our thoughts and situations are surely different, but if we spend time working together, especially using our hands, even at simple tasks, which small children should be welcomed to be involved in, we can learn new viewpoints and develop compassion for each other. Because we have real communication that includes the environment, animals, plants, and other creatures, we can access more and deeper insights and get support and help from each other. Each of these elements has their own spirit, and they are communicating with each other all the time. Humans may be the only species that has forgotten about the connection to all living things and lost the great benefit and potential to live at ease in a richer and more creative way.

FIRE FESTIVAL FOR BROTHERHOOD AND INITIATION

Dōsojin Hi-matsuri is a fire festival held on January 15 every year. It is one of Japan's three major fire festivals. *Dōsojin* are a couple of Shinto deities, who are believed to protect crossroads, mountain passes, village boundaries, and travelers from evil spirits. They are also worshiped for fertility and children's healthy growth. The *Dōsojin* fire festival is more than 200 years old and has been passed down for generations in the village of Nozawa Onsen in the Nagano prefecture. The village is in a mountainous area well known for snow and hot springs. On January 15, the day of the fire festival, the village is covered by deep snow.

The festival is an act of dynamic enactment: the forty-two- and twenty-five-year-old males of the village are supposed to defend a twenty-three-foot-high shrine against the rest of the villagers who rush toward it with flaming torches. Forty-two- and twenty-five-year-olds are chosen because those ages for males are said to be *yakudoshi*, ages of misfortunate in Japanese Shinto beliefs. By defending the shrine, which they build the day before the festival, for *Dōsojin* using a special kind of wood from trees they cut down in the mountain during October, the males are defending themselves from bad fortune and praying for strength to protect females and their fertility.

In 2023, I visited the village to observe the famous fire festival in snow. I had only the basic knowledge you can get on the internet or in travel guidebooks, and some curiosity to experience the cultural heritage of my native country. It turned out the festival I participated in was much more spectacular and sacred than I had ever imagined.

The battle of fire between the defenders and offenders—the rest of the villagers, mostly male—lasted three hours. The defenders stood in front of the shrine and frantically worked to prevent the offenders from getting to the shrine to set it on fire with burning torches. I was standing in the second line close to the battle, and I had to cover my hair, shoulders, and sleeves from sparks leaping from the torches.

Finally, after hundreds of attempts and battles, the shrine caught fire and started to burn. The wooden shrine made of *buna* beech tree, which was still moist, was burning slowly but surely with the increasing power of the flames. At the very last moment before the shrine came crashing down to the ground, the gigantic flame flared up as if the fire of *Dōsojin*, the united male and female couple deity, reached up to the sky. It was, indeed, the grand finale.

I had never seen an initiation ritual before. I had little knowledge about initiation other than it is a rite of passage marking entrance into adulthood or beginning something new, and typically has its own ritual. The fire festival was, indeed, a ritual, which I would have never experienced if I had not gone to the village and watched the festival in front of me. It was an initiation for twenty-five-year-olds who were becoming adults and forty-two-year-olds becoming new authorities in the village. They had to be approved by other villagers and the spirit of *Dōsojin*, and through the serious battles with fire, their souls were purged.

Battles were among males, but they were under the watchful eyes of the females and children of the village.

After the shrine crashed to the ground, I saw groups of males of different ages putting their arms around each other while still looking at the fire. Their smiles were beaming with satisfaction, accomplishment, confidence, and, perhaps, with new hope for the years to come. It was a beautiful scene, and I was very grateful to participate in such a sacred event.

Challenges and struggles are there to help us learn to overcome obstacles and grow to the next level of our development. Those who have gone through difficulties before can lead, teach, and support you. It is the family bond you can rely on that shows you how to build the core strength of believing in yourself and something greater than you can grasp in your mind.

DIVINE FEMININE, THE SACRED CREATIVITY

Simply defined, I believe sisterhood is for developing creativity and brotherhood is for gaining the strength to protect creativity. When your creativity is cultivated with the help and support from other people and the spirits of other elements, a metamorphosis takes place within you and your creative power becomes sacred, which is the principle of the divine feminine.

Divine feminine energy exists in all of us, both male and female. I will talk about divine feminine more later. I simply mention it here in the context of our creativity. It is your nurturing, receptive, compassionate, and inclusive energy. Divine feminine energy can influence the way our society functions so people are more forgiving and understanding of each other.

You can tap into your divine feminine energy by honoring your universal mother: Mother Earth, Mother Ocean, Mother Nature, and the Mother of the Universe, who care about you deeply and are always there to help you. Sisterhood and brotherhood are the communion to evoke your inner calling to your Universal Mother. In Hawaiian words, it is *mana*, the power and strength that reside within you and within everything around you.

Below, I have listed five activities that will help you connect to your divine feminine energy through sisterhood/brotherhood and develop your creativity to be more accessible and have a greater effect.

1. **Gather in nature:** Plan to gather outdoors for sisterhood or brotherhood. Participants are supposed to be female only for sisterhood and male only for brotherhood. That way, you can relate to each other more easily without any competitive thoughts, and you feel safer and more relaxed. I recommend gathering outside because open space can help you feel free, you most likely get more insights from elements in nature, and you naturally get access to your *mana*.

2. **Do some work with others:** When you work with others, not only do you get things accomplished easier, but it is also much more enjoyable to work with other people. The result is the work does not feel like a burden or hardship anymore, and you will start seeing work with a brand-new perspective as something with a higher purpose, and once you accomplish the job, it will give you great joy.

3. **Celebrate and give rewards to each other:** Celebration is a wonderful way to reflect on what you have been through and to visualize who you want to be in the future. If you celebrate in sisterhood/brotherhood, you naturally feel happy for each other and grow stronger bonds with them. Their existence itself may be your biggest reward.

4. **Sit around the table and eat together:** You will realize that food tastes better if you eat with a group of people, especially after you work as a team together. Having conversations in a relaxed environment and enjoying good food helps you appreciate your good health and peaceful situation. Joy, appreciation, and peace are the feelings you want to maintain to live healthily and be fulfilled.

5. **Put a smile on your face:** A smile is your best dress. It is as simple as that. If you want to be around people who are smiling, smile first. Your smile attracts other smiles.

EXERCISE

1. Create a gathering you can have regularly with a group of women if you are a woman or men if you are a man. Think of a location somewhere outside and work you would enjoy doing with others. You may join an existing group if you find one doing activities involving some hand work outside. Write down where and what kind of work you are going to do below.

____

____

____

____

____

2. When you choose a group activity and a location, think of yourself in that situation. What kind of people will be there? Do they resonate with the location and the work? Are you comfortable with them? When you form a group of people, it is better if you start with a small group of friends, and as the group grows, you can start inviting other people, but keep it limited to people you and your friends know. That way, you can maintain a safe and relaxing group environment. Write down a list of friends you would like to form a group with.

---

3. If you do not feel like forming a group of sisters/brothers by yourself, look for a group that already exists and ask them if you can join. Write down the potential sisterhood/brotherhood group and the name of its contact person below.

---

4. Do some simple, short meditation. Close your eyes, exhale love out and inhale love in, and imagine every single cell of your body has a smiley face, from the tip of your toes to the top of your head. Remember, if you want smiling people around you, you should radiate big smiles. Draw a smiley face below.

SUMMARY

Back in the old days, people lived in communities with strong ties. We used to have good support systems naturally, learned from elders. We worked together, including with children, had meals together, and performed ceremonies together. In modern days, it is more difficult to maintain the same connection with each other. We spend lots of time inside, away from nature and others. We mostly use our brains and do much less physical work. Living this way, it is not easy to feel the warmth of other people—the warmth of their bodies and their hearts.

Sisterhood/brotherhood is an excellent way to be brought back to how humans lived back in the old days. We are creatures of community. A community can exist in any form, including family, neighbors, school, clubs, and so on. We feel safest when we are secured and protected by others and can feel the warmth of other people's hearts. In the community, we develop sisterhood/brotherhood and we support each other, work together, solve problems together, and raise children together. Warmth in our heart nourishes us and gives us strength.

Chapter 6

Making Your Family a Priority

"Family faces are magic mirrors.
Looking at people who belong to us,
we see the past, present, and future."

— Grail Lumet Buckley

In the last chapter, we talked about the importance of having a safe and comfortable sisterhood/brotherhood where you can relate to and support each other. The issue may be we do not know how to open our heart to others, trust others, and feel safe enough to express what we are really thinking and who we really are. Our parents, caregivers, and others who raised us influenced our thoughts and mind patterns from an early age, making it difficult to see what *we* are really thinking and feeling. Our true self is often hidden underneath many layers of our parents/caregivers' values, patterns, and other influences.

We were taught how to behave and how to think, and often even how to feel. Many of us grew up in our busy, modern society isolated by our family and not given enough chances to really feel what our bodily sensations were, what we really like, or what we really want to do. Choices were made for us too quickly, before we actually had a chance to understand what they meant.

Vulnerable infants who rely on their caregiver, who is often their mother, pick up everything from this person who is fundamental to their survival. So, as an infant, we had no choice but to listen, look, and respond to our caregiver.

We quickly develop a sensitivity to our mother/caregiver. We recognize their tone of voice, their impressions of the world, and pay attention to their mood innately. We were naturally connected to our mother or closest caregiver since before we had a conscious mind. Our feelings, mindset, and habitual thinking are embedded in our subconscious, and they were programmed by our mother or caregiver.

In this chapter, let's talk about how to reveal your true self by getting to know your family from a deeper perspective.

How did you feel about your family or the closest adults when you were growing up? Did you like them? What kinds of memories do you have with them? Do those memories make you feel happy or sad? Whatever your feelings toward your family, you can learn a lot about yourself by knowing your family. The more you look at them, the more you will see yourself. Family is your treasure chest filled with gold, jewels, and all sorts of precious things that can fulfill your need to go on your hero/ heroine's journey to find love in yourself.

MOTHER'S INFLUENCE

Growing up, my mother often used to tell me, "Don't get married to a guy who takes you far away. Be sure you stay close to your home." Contrary to my mother's hope, around the age six, I started developing my dream to leave Japan and explore the vast world across the ocean.

My mother grew up on a small island off the island of Kyushu. This remote island has a population of only 30,000, and its main industry is fishing and farming. When she was a teenager, my mother wanted to get off the island and away from country living. She told me she was tired of living with her father, who was such an austere person. The remote area was steeped in tradition, which she found too rigid, and the community and family ties were too tight. She felt she was caught in the small net of the society and her family.

At fifteen, she decided to leave the island and move to Nagoya, the third biggest city in Japan. She worked as a nurse's assistant at a clinic during the day and went to school at night. Right after graduating from high school, she met my father and married him when she was twenty. She married into a big household—grandfather-in-law, grandmother-in-law, father-in-law, and stepmother-in-law. Her stepmother-in-law used to be my grandfather's mistress. When my father's real mother passed away while he was in college, the mistress became his father's wife, his stepmother. I imagine this was a time when our family's fate got twisted in a complicated way.

I had no way of knowing what it was when I was little, but our family atmosphere had a heaviness I can now define as that of sadness and family secrets. As a little girl, I subconsciously felt some sort of message from my mother when she told me not to marry and move far away from home. It was her asking for help. It was her way of putting her sadness and pressure aside in the hope her daughter would stay close and grow up to understand and be compassionate to her mother.

I was my parents' first child and the first grandchild to my grandparents. I grew up surrounded by three generations of adults: parents, grandparents, and great-grandparents. I grew up with adults nearby. In my case, I had the closest connection physically and mentally with my mother.

My mother was never allowed to work. My father is a kindhearted man with a gentle manner, but he is very protective and conservative. He grew up as the first son of the family. In our culture, especially for his generation (he was born during World War II), the eldest son was born to carry responsibility and take pride as the heir of the bloodline. It was a matter of pride for him to bring home sufficient income so his wife could stay home, and it was also his responsibility to take good care of the whole family. My mother stayed home, did all the errands, and looked after her children and elders at home as she was obliged to. She did so because she thought she had to give up her own will to care for the family, so she did. She gave up her freedom, independence, and passion.

I was her girl, her hope, and her love, but I knew I was not her doll.

I grew up under the influence of my mother's emotional instability. She had mood swings, she would get frustrated and upset without reason, and often, her negative emotions were unleashed on her daughter. I often cried because of her mean words and unreasonable accusations—she would say I was a bad girl for no reason. I strived to be a good student to make my mother happy. I learned to act fine when I was sick to keep my mother from worrying about me.

LEAVING HOME

Did you leave your parents' home when you became an adult, or did you stay home? If you stayed home, have you ever regretted it? If you regret staying home because you faced restrictions despite your will, you can still spread your wings and fly.

I was not allowed to go to the university because my father said girls should never be smarter than boys. I had to listen to him, so I went to a two-year college. When I graduated, I looked for a job. I wanted to work for a travel agency because it was my dream to go beyond Japan. My father said no. Once again, I had to follow his order to work for a financial institute, even though I had zero interest in the financial field, and to keep looking for a husband who could earn a good salary. My father believed having a husband with a good salary was how his daughter would have a happy life.

Even after I became a legal adult, I still had a curfew and was never allowed to live by myself.

I met my husband at work, and I got married at twenty-three. It was my only way to get out of the family. My husband then took a job at an office in Beijing, China. We started our wedded life in Beijing just five years after the Tiananmen Square Massacre. A year later, I had my son, Kei. Eleven years later, I got divorced while we were living in Taiwan. Later, we'll talk in more detail about that part of my life's journey.

I took Kei, and I met my second husband in the San Francisco Bay Area, in California. I started my life in the United States—the country I dreamed of as the land for freedom. Nine years later, my second husband died from brain cancer. With a heart full of grief, I decided to start my new chapter in a new land, the island of Maui, Hawaii. I moved by myself, started a food company, bought land with a house, and planted various fruit trees to make the place an organic farm and healing sanctuary. I got a permit to run a bed and breakfast and catered mostly to women who came to Maui for retreats.

After COVID-19 hit, I felt it was time to sell the bed and breakfast and two-acre organic farm. Around the same time, my father got cancer back in Japan, which made me rethink my life and my love for my family. When I sold my farm on Maui, I decided to split my time between Maui and my hometown in Japan. Here I was, once again close to my parents, but this time it was different from when I left my family home thirty years ago. I am now about to start my new project, which is to work for the divine feminine principle and help women work toward freedom, independence, and self-love.

MEMORIES OF LOVE

Despite complicated family dynamics, I must admit my parents made great efforts to provide their children with a happy family. I remember picnic lunches under cherry blossom trees every spring. My mother's *tamagoyaki* and *onigiri* were the best foods in the world. Every summer, we had a family trip to the beach, and that's where I learned how to swim. We went to hot springs every winter. We took a bath in naturally mineral-rich, warm water several times a day and played card games together after the bath. I can see my mother's smile in every scene in those memories.

I want to share a story about a general in Myanmar, where a political battle raged for many years. The general was kept in a military prison for more than twenty years. After he was released, he was interviewed about how he had managed his difficult life in a prison cell.

The interviewer asked, "How were you able to stay sane? How did you maintain your inner peace?"

The general answered, "It was really, really hard to be kept in the solitary cell, where there was no window, no clean toilet, nobody to talk to, nothing to read or write…. There I spent days and days remembering my wife's face. I visualized the wrinkles on her face slowly, one by one, every single stroke. That was what kept me alive. Memories of her love, memories of our love."

I was stunned by his story. What nourishes your soul is love. The richness of your life is about how many memories of love you have.

Now I know I am grateful for my parents because they gave me bright memories of love in the family.

GREAT-GRANDMOTHER AS REPRESENTATIVE GENERATION

My great-grandmother was born in 1893. That year, the Panic of 1893 happened when the New York Stock Exchange crashed, marking the beginning of a depression. It was also when the Kingdom of Hawaii was overthrown, and the United States took it over. In Japan, the next year saw the beginning of the first Sino-Japanese War with China, which was followed by the Russo-Japanese War with Russia. The woolen textile industry was flourishing in the area where she was born and raised because a big river ran through the area, and an abundance of water was necessary for wool manufacturing.

She had a financially comfortable childhood because her father was a successful wool manufacturer. Her marriage to my great-grandfather was arranged, which was common at the time in Japan, and she gave birth to and raised seven children. It was a time when the world was running toward wars, and Japan was going through major changes, as was she.

The war changed everything in the country, including the lives of citizens. My great-grandfather had inherited the family business, an inn along the major road between north and south Japan, but through the wars between China and Russia, and new development throughout the country, a new road was built bypassing the inn, so it was no longer at a confluence for travelers. This was the end of their business. After that, and after he came back from the war with Russia, he lost interest in business and everyday mundane things, so it was up to my great-grandmother to feed her seven children.

She started a bathhouse. I have asked around, but no one in the family knows where she got the idea. In the early 1900s, many if not most households in Japan had no shower or bath, so her new bathhouse was packed every day, and the business went well. My grandfather took it over when he became an adult. I remember when I was little, I sat at the reception counter with my step-grandmother and watched both the men's side and women's side. Naturally, I observed the various human body shapes without prejudice or judgment at such a young age. To my little girl's eyes, they looked relaxed and refreshed, and it left a quite nice, peaceful impression.

After World War II, and as the new economy developed, people started installing their own baths at home. Naturally, my father closed the bathhouse and chose a completely different profession.

My great-grandmother worked at the bath house into her late eighties. She was known as a hardworking and strong woman by the family. I cannot recall her smiling face; instead, I remember her sitting next to the *hibachi* (fire bowl) that contained burning charcoal and always knitting. She made several pairs of shorts for me to keep me warm in winter. My mother helped me put them on before I went to preschool on cold winter mornings. This fond memory of the warmth my great-grandmother provided has stayed with me.

Forty years after my great-grandmother's death, the generations have shifted. My parents are getting close to the age I remember her being, and I, her first great-grandchild, am becoming the successor of the bloodline.

Recently, I had a strong pull to learn more about my great-grandmother's origins. I tracked down her father's wool manufacturing business and found it was still in operation in a modern way. I went there several times to weave and made a scarf, as I mentioned in Chapter 4. I wear the scarf I made at her birthplace—it is my way of remembering her and respecting her way of making a living to keep her family and the following generations alive. Now I understand and sympathize with her. Perhaps she wished to live differently as a woman, be protected, and focus on being a kind and gentle mother and mother-in-law, but she did not have that choice. She had to be a fighter and became a business-minded woman with a stern face.

I often think about how many women have existed who, like my great-grandmother, live through great difficulties, especially wars, and how they influenced the following generations. I feel her DNA in me since I have myself started my own business and spent exhausting days multitasking. After I let go of my urge to keep my business running successfully, I can now take a deep breath. I am awed by and grateful for whatever made me realize who I am and who I want to be. I feel my great-grandmother's spirit guiding me to this day, helping me stand strong with love for my family, and most importantly, for myself.

FINDING MY SOUL THROUGH MY FATHER

When my father was diagnosed with cancer in the winter of 2021, he was hospitalized and went through a difficult surgery. I was unable to go back to Japan because of COVID-19 restrictions. Every day, I desperately prayed for his safe and successful surgery. I did not want him to die yet. I felt like I owed him something, as if I had some mission to work on. I am still not sure what it was, and I may never figure it out. I just felt I couldn't let him go yet. I wanted him to feel he'd had a good life, to feel he was surrounded by love and embraced by care, and not to feel lonely.

I felt on some level like I was being asked by his mother, who had suddenly passed away when he was in college, to let him know he was loved by her more than he remembers. She is my grandmother, but I never met her because she died before my parents met. I have no way to find out what was in her mind when she left her physical body early—she was only fifty. I can only imagine how sorry she was to leave her family, especially her children—how worried her spirit must have been and must be still, and her spirit remains in my blood. I am connected to her spirit, yet I live my life with my own soul. I believe it must be her spirit's wish for me to find my own individuality and happiness, which is also to help her child, my father, but not to sacrifice my own soul. I believe it is my mission to clear my family karma and install a new tradition and new way of peace for my child and my future grandchildren. That is why I am back in my family home and living the art of love.

MAKING YOUR LOVED ONES A PRIORITY

Here are five ways I make my loved ones a priority. I believe you too will achieve success in this area if you follow these practices.

1. **Set up a routine of making a phone or video call with them:** Do it every week, every three days, or whatever time interval you are comfortable with, and stick with it.

2. **Visit them, sit with them, and have meals with them as often as you can:** You can make each visit enjoyable by looking at it from a higher perspective within your soul. You will soon find the more time you spend with them, the more they will open up to you and you will hear more stories about yourself as a child, about your ancestors, and about your family history. This is a treasure box for you while taking your heroine/hero's journey.

3. **Ask them to show you pictures of when you were a newborn:** When you see yourself as a tiny infant embraced by your parents, you will notice how happy they look holding you. You will see the love they have in their eyes, and how bright the lights are surrounding them as new parents welcoming you to this world. You will realize you are the most precious thing in the entire world for them, and your existence itself makes them the happiest humans on earth.

4. **Ask how they are and let them speak:** Be a good listener. An old Japanese quote says: "A shop-boy near the temple gate will recite

sutras untaught." You learn from what you hear without realizing you are learning.

5. **Pray for them:** Remember you are creating your own reality, and you have the power to change your reality. By giving your prayers, you are sending your positive message for them to the universe, and it will respond to your message.

EXERCISE

1. Which five people in your life are your top priority?

2. What do you do daily to actively nourish your relationship with these five people?

3. Which of these five people have you not reached out to often or recently enough?

____

____

____

____

4. What action will you commit to taking to get in touch with these five people and spend more time with them?

____

____

____

____

SUMMARY

Knowing is the first step to forgiving. To know and understand deeply, you need to look at the people who inspire strong feelings, either positive or negative. By looking at the people who most influenced you, often your family, you find out what you learned from them from birth onward and find you learned some things even before you had a conscious mind. As you simply get in touch with yourself as a vulnerable infant, you will feel deep sympathy for your inner child, and that is the key to opening the door to connecting consciousness to your root, to your heart, and to your spirit. In doing so, you will be able to forgive others. Even though you might not agree with the way your parents raised you, it was the best they could do with what they knew, the way they were brought up, and with what society and culture were like in their time. It is okay to love them. I assure you, loving them unconditionally will be immensely healing for you.

Chapter 7

Connecting to Your Divine Feminine and Masculine

"All these things he will do out of ignorance of the Law,

and as a man dying slowly cannot smell his own stench,

so will the Son of Man be blind to the truth:

that as he plunders and ravages and destroys his Earthly Mother,

so does he plunder and ravage and destroy himself.

For he was born of his Earthly Mother,

and he is one with her,

and all that he does to his Mother even so does he do to himself."

— *The Fourth Gospel of the Essenes*, translated from Aramaic by Edmund Szekely

The masculine and feminine archetypes are represented often by a god and goddess image all over the world, including in the West, Sumer, India, Egypt, and throughout

Asia. The Venus of Willendorf is a figure of the goddess Venus, who is the goddess of love and beauty. This goddess archetype originated with Ishtar in Sumer and syncretized to Aphrodite in Greek and Venus in Roman mythology. The Venus of Willendorf is made of limestone. It was found in a cave at a Paleolithic site in Austria, and it is estimated to have been made 30,000 years ago.

Through much of human history since around 1500 BCE, in most places we've lived in a world dominated and ruled by the masculine archetype, suppressing the feminine archetype, whose principle is to embrace, unite, and nurture to find balance. As a result of this lack of balance between masculinity and femininity, we see many instances of separation and division—separation between races, religions, and countries, and division between rich and poor, male and female, children and adults, human and other creatures, made and natural materials, and mind and soul. The law written in the *Fourth Gospel of the Essenes* gives us an exact description of what is going on in our current society.

In the previous chapter, we talked about forgiveness. Knowing is the first step in forgiveness, and it is the very quality of the feminine archetype. Let's look at these qualities of femininity—the divine feminine—to clearly see why it is crucial for us to regain these qualities by connecting to our divine feminine today.

DIVINE FEMININE IN PREHISTORIC CULTURE

Archaeological evidence indicates ancient civilizations in various areas worshiped goddesses, such as Inanna in Sumer, Lakshmi in the Indus River Valley, Isis in Egypt, and Guanyin in China, from the beginning of their civilizations.

Small humanoid figures made of clay have been found in different archaeological sites of the Jomon period in Japan. Those figures are called *Dogū*, and they are found exclusively in Jomon sites, none from any sites following the Jomon period, which is 14,000 to 300 BCE in prehistoric Japan. Most of *Dogū* appear to be female, and they are considered representative of goddesses. Many are specifically mother goddesses since they have large abdomens associated with pregnancy, and scholars consider people in the Jomo period made *Dogū* for fertility and shamanistic rites.

The Jomon period started by 14,000 BCE and lasted more than 13,000 years, which is more than three times longer than the time between the construction of the pyramid of Giza in Egypt and today. People in the Jomon period lived mostly as hunter-gathers, eating tree nuts and catching fish and clams. They had a rich culture, made pottery, and held ceremonial rituals using *Dogū*. Sedentism, which refers to living in settlements, started during the Jomon culture in Japan, and people lived in large groups for long periods, which was rare in hunter-gatherer times— evidence of such settlements this early have only been found in North America other than during the Jomon period in Japan.[1] Scholars believe these communities developed because the humans in

---

1 Dow, Gregory K. and Clyde G. Reed. "The Origins of Sedentism: Climate, Population, and Technology." *Journal of Economic Behavior & Organization.* 119 (2015): 56-71. https://www.sciencedirect.com/science/article/pii/S0167268115001985. Accessed December 1, 2023.

the Jomon period lived in harmony with nature, planted trees with nuts, grew some beans, and lived close to the shore to fish.

Another interesting fact about the Jomon period is none of the weapons nor human remains found in the sites show traces of battle. That means humans in the Jomon period did not have battles between tribes, they did not harm each other, and they were living in peace. This was a period when we humans were in harmony with nature and lived in peace with each other for 13,000 years.

My question is: Why was it possible for humans in the Jomon period of pre-history to live in harmony with nature and in peace with other people, and not for us modern humans? Why did *Dogū* and other ceremonial pottery disappear after the Jomon period? If *Dogū* were made to worship mother goddesses by Jomon people, why didn't we continue? When did we start separating ourselves from nature, dividing ourselves from each other, and losing the awareness that all life is sacred?

MOTHER GODDESS WITHIN YOU

Research shows that not only during the Jomon period in Japan, but all over the world in the Paleolithic and Neolithic periods, the principal deity worshipped was a mother goddess—no creator beyond her creation. All species were her children, and everything on the planet and beyond was connected through her.

Around 1500 BCE, the story of the Garden of Eden, as told in Genesis, elevated humans as a special species above any other creatures on earth and created by a creator god, seen as the Father. Eve, the first female, did something sinful by eating a forbidden fruit from the tree of knowledge, thus the ensuing human fate of suffering began.

I do not know for sure when the mother goddess disappeared; she isn't in the Garden of Eden. With this new creation story, humans started carrying the burden of sin and were destined to live in fear of the Creator's anger and punishment.

The influence of Genesis has been enormous, and ever since, our history reflects the loss of the mother goddess, unconditional love, the unification of all life, and communion with the spirits around and within us. Our history became the history of constant wars spurred by greed and the development of our society's focus on materialistic abundance and selfish individualism, which we win through severe and endless competition and the neglect and destruction of nature.

When will we realize that in harming and suppressing our mothers—Mother Nature, Mother Earth, Mother Ocean, and our own motherhood, which we, both male and female, have within ourselves—we are harming ourselves? We cannot nurture ourselves without motherhood, which embodies the caring, giving, accepting, and unconditionally loving qualities inside all of us.

BATHING IN RIVER NILE

The River Nile has been called the tears of Isis in Egypt since ancient times. The myth is that when the Goddess Isis mourned the death of her beloved husband Osiris, she shed so many tears that the Nile flooded. The flood destroyed towns and houses, and at the same time, it cleansed the earth and made the land fertile.

I wanted to see the Nile River, the tears of Isis, which is one of the biggest reasons I went to visit Egypt. Written human history began in Mesopotamia (cuneiform) and then Egypt (hieroglyphics) around 3200 BCE. Egyptian civilization contributed directly to Greek and Roman civilizations. Isis was the primary goddess in Egypt. She was believed to help the dead enter the afterlife as she had helped Osiris, and she was considered the divine mother of pharaoh because she was the mother of Horus, the deity of kingship, healing, protection, the sun, and the sky.

Before I went to Egypt, I had no idea what it is like to live in the desert, where the air is so dry, everything is predominantly brown, and the sun's glare feels so intense. The River Nile, which runs through the desert, creates green areas along its banks and provides moisture and cools the air. I went on a cruise and saw villages along the river; I saw kids swimming, women washing clothes at the shore, and villagers bathing livestock. The people's lives were intertwined with the river, and looking at them, I felt nostalgic, as if I remembered those days, even though I never experienced them or saw them in this lifetime anywhere else.

One afternoon in mid-May, I was visiting Luxor, a town about 400 miles south of Cairo, and I stayed at a little hotel along the Nile. I took a boat with a group of women to a little island off the shore about twenty minutes away from the boat dock. We could swim in the river there. We were told it was not advised for tourists to swim in the Nile because we might encounter crocodiles or risk exposure to certain parasites, and we understood women in Egypt do not expose their skin nor their body shape, wear swimsuits, nor swim in public because of their religious beliefs. A special arrangement was made for us, and the boat took us to a spot where we were not widely exposed to public eyes.

We got off the boat on the island when the sun was leaning toward the horizon. The water's surface reflected the sun, turning the water cobalt blue with a touch of orange. The water was clear, and the current looked fast toward the middle but gentle by the shore. I took off my sandals on the beach and put my feet in the water; it was cold. In contrast to the intense heat in the air, the water in the River Nile felt icy cold.

Slowly, inch by inch, I walked into the water. I realized it was cold, but it somehow felt soft. My skin was absorbing the water as if it were satisfying a thirst, and my body was relaxed. I was enjoying being in the water, and it no longer felt cold. I felt the presence of gentleness, which was hard to put into words, as if I were within some deep sense of knowingness that was telling me it was okay to just be there. In the moment, I felt like I was being embraced and cradled in the arms of the river spirit, the spirit of mother goddess, of Isis, the Divine Mother, or whatever you wish to name her. It was the wonderful secure feeling of being fully accepted by being present as who I am.

After a while, I got out of the river and walked up to the beach. As soon as I started walking toward my sandals, I felt a hot breeze, as if someone were making a bonfire nearby. But there was no fire; instead, the magnificent reddish orange sun was approaching the horizon behind the shadows of houses across the river. The hot breeze was created by the heat of the sun, as if it were burning. My body, which was soaking wet from the cold river water, dried in the hot breeze instantly. I felt the presence of the father god, who can expose you in strongly focused heat and spur you into action immediately. My heart was filled with gratitude for both soothing mother energy and driving father energy, and that is when I understood we need both the divine feminine and divine masculine.

Through my experience in Egypt, I learned through my bodily sensations in nature that we should strive to cultivate divine feminine and divine masculine balance in harmony. I think it is easier to understand it by experiencing it and feeling it with your body and heart than studying it and thinking about it in your mind.

MOTHERHOOD AND FATHERHOOD

We live in a world where masculine energy, which is often misunderstood and distorted from divine masculine, dominates the society as a result of suppressing the divine feminine. I believe developing the divine feminine in each one of us, both female and male, can give us strength. We can refine our society to live in unity with our planet and all life and have the strength to believe in our ability to love and nurture—and to live in peace.

How do you define motherhood and fatherhood? By accessing both motherhood and fatherhood within yourself, which naturally invokes images of the positive aspects of feminine and masculine, you will better understand what the divine feminine means. Below is a list of the four things you need to access your inner motherhood and fatherhood.

1. **Determine what motherhood is for you:** Mother is the one who created you, nurtured you, and loves you unconditionally. The difference between the Divine Mother and a human mother is a human mother has a physical body, and she has sensuality and sexuality so she can create and give birth to you. The Divine Mother is not a person but the mother aspect of God. Mother accepts you no matter who and how you are with no judgment, and she is always there for you.

2. **Determine what fatherhood is for you:** Father is the one who distinguishes danger and protects you from it. To do so, instead of being in fighting mode all the time with whoever is around, he needs wisdom, power, and confidence. Father has deep love and respect for your mother and appreciates her beauty and caring nature. He knows without her there is no sky nor sun in the world nor would he exist if he hadn't been given birth to by his own mother.

3. **Contemplate your thoughts:** Are motherhood or fatherhood qualities lacking within you? I personally feel my fatherhood quality is somewhat missing, which is natural because I am a woman, and I have more of the motherhood quality. I am a mother to my son

and have developed mother qualities by raising a child. Because I know I am lacking in fatherhood energy, I am working on it to help understand and cultivate it. You, too, by realizing which quality you lack, can work on it and have both in balance, which will benefit you and your loved ones.

4. **Achieve balance:** Divine feminine is to have both motherhood and fatherhood in balance within you. It is having balance and an inclusive aspect, which unites with other people and with nature, and creates flow by communicating through heart and senses. It overrules male or female dominance. It is the unification of yin and yang, which transforms and creates a new thing, a new reality, a new world.

EXERCISE

1. Think about your mother or your ideal mother and write down the qualities she has that you admire.

____

____

____

____

____

____

2. Think about your father or your ideal father and write down the qualities he has that you admire.

____

____

____

____

____

____

____

3. Which qualities that you wrote down above about mothers and fathers are you missing?

____

____

____

____

____

____

4. Were the qualities you wrote down in number three more from mothers or fathers?

    ____

    ____

5. Hold the image of your ideal mother or father, whichever quality you are missing more, and embrace it. Knowing what you are missing is the first step in healing. Embrace your inner mother or inner father, and write down how you feel now.

    ____

    ____

    ____

    ____

    ____

    ____

6. If negative feelings toward your mother or father come up, write about the feelings on a separate piece of paper. Then tear the paper into small pieces and burn it.

SUMMARY

The divine feminine is a big subject, and we all share a long history of it being suppressed, distorted, and abused. We are living in a world with so many problems—war, poverty, misinformation, a food crisis, a health crisis, and environmental destruction. How can we raise our children to believe their future is bright if the world they see is filled with anger, fighting, poverty, illness, and hunger—a world where it seems we are always busy and unsatisfied? We must work on healing our inner motherhood and fatherhood and find a way to embrace the divine feminine within each of us. By cultivating it, I believe we can remember how good we are and how much love each of us is carrying within and for others.

Chapter 8

Coping with Grief

"You can't truly heal from a loss until you
allow yourself to really feel the loss."

— Mandy Hale

No one wants to experience grief; however, everyone encounters it at some point to a certain degree. When the loss is too painful, it can be difficult to access your feelings. Over time, little by little, you can reach your hidden feelings if you are patient with yourself and give yourself enough strength to allow your emotions to be released. Then you can truly heal from the loss.

As discussed in the last chapter, one of the divine feminine qualities is to have compassion for others. Let's focus on one particular feeling—grief—in this chapter. Having compassion for yourself is fundamentally important for you to heal from grief.

GRIEVING IS THE PROCESS OF ACCEPTING PAIN

Grief is the feeling of loss. It is commonly understood that someone will grieve after the loss caused by the death of a loved one, including a parent, sibling, spouse, child, or best friend. Grief can be felt not only by the death of loved ones, but also by the loss of a pet, job, or home, or any other significant loss, and it often occurs as a result of divorce.

Grief can be felt through many different emotions, such as depression, sadness, anger, anxiety, and even guilt. The degree of grief depends on each individual's situation and personality, and the grieving process can take a long time before the person heals.

I have experienced both divorce (from my first marriage) and the death of my spouse (from my second marriage). Now, almost nine years after the death of my second husband, I have a clearer view of what was really going on in my grieving process in both situations.

When I got divorced from my first husband, I was extremely tired. I was married to him for eleven years and had Kei with him. Early in the marriage, I realized something was wrong in our relationship, but I denied my feelings for a long time. He is the father of my precious child, and the idea of separating my child from his father terrified me. I wanted to be separated from my husband, but it took me several years to build up my self-confidence to have the courage to break through the Japanese cultural moral belief that divorce is taboo. Plus, I would have social disadvantages as a single mother and lose my parents' support because they would criticize me as an irresponsible mother to their grandson.

Shortly after my divorce, I took Kei to America to start our new lives. I felt it would be almost impossible to raise Kei the way I wanted if we stayed in an environment of cultural prejudice and limitations. In California, I met Graham. We immediately felt a strong attraction to each other and were married within a year.

Graham helped Kei and I become accustomed to our new culture and the different language and to meet new family members and friends. We went skiing and hiking, had barbeques in the backyard, and spent wonderful years enjoying our family life together. During this time, I did not think much about my previous marriage or life in Japan and other parts of the world. I dove into my new life and was busy raising my child to become a smart, kind, and caring person who knows what love feels like. Plus, I had my career, which gave me fulfilment and self-worth.

Now, after almost ten years, I can analyze what was going on in my life at that time. Back then, I never thought it was important for me to grasp what was happening in my heart and thoughts beneath the surface of my day-to-day life.

Unconsciously, I was afraid to look back at my past. I had disappointment and a broken heart from the man to whom I had once vowed forever love. I also was disappointed that my parents did not give me mental support in my divorce. I did not pay attention to my grief, which was caused by the loss of the relationship with my once trusted spouse, the end of my dream to raise a happy family, and the failure of my dream of my parents opening their arms and accepting me no matter what situation I was in. I was sad and angry, and I felt defeated. I kept feeling like I was a loser, despite the happy married life I was establishing with my wonderful new husband.

I did not want to feel the painful negative emotions from my divorce. To forget the painful past and keep moving forward, I neglected the heaviness I kept in my heart. I did not dare to see that I was still grieving even after I had started my new life. If I had really paid attention to what I was feeling deep inside my heart and I had dealt with my grief from my divorce, I would have had a different way of coping with the next grief I experienced when Graham died.

BE TENDER TO YOURSELF

Seven years into our marriage, Graham was diagnosed with brain cancer. He passed away twenty months after that. During those twenty months, after the doctor told us to organize our lives and be ready for Graham's departure to the other realm, I am not sure how I kept myself strong. I lived day by day without giving any thought to my future without Graham. I only remember thinking, "This is way too hard to handle, but I have no choice but just to do it." When Graham passed away, even though I'd had twenty months to prepare for his death, I was not ready.

I went back to work one month after Graham's death. I preferred to be busy. I kept myself occupied with my routine, commuting and working at the office in San Francisco. I had my girlfriends come over for dinner during weekends. I also started my meditation practice, learned reiki, and practiced macrobiotic cooking, which is a form of health-conscious eating. I occupied my thoughts by working or doing something I enjoyed. I only cried sometimes, and I thought that was because I was okay.

At the time, one of my girlfriends told me that losing your loved one is like having a hole in your heart. People say it will heal over time, but that is not true; it is never going to heal. Instead, you learn to live with a hole in your heart. My girlfriend was right.

In the years after Graham's passing, I followed many spiritual practices, including different meditation methods, energy work, reiki, past life regression, and mantra chanting. I continue my practices to this day. I thought about what the meaning of Graham and me meeting each other was, and why he got a serious illness and died. Nobody, including me, could tell me what lesson I was supposed to learn from his death, or what mission in life I was to accomplish as the result of experiencing the tremendous pain of losing him.

I had many feelings when I lost him. I was very sad and somewhat lost. I also felt guilty. At first, I felt guilty because I thought he had continued to undergo some severe treatments for my sake, and they may have caused him to suffer more. As I calmed down, I blamed myself less for his treatments, but I was unable to shake the guilt. Finally, I realized the guilt was caused by wondering whether I had been fully there and truly myself in our relationship. I realized, during our marriage I had held on to my negative feelings and resentment about my divorce, my parents, and Japanese society. I hid those feelings deep inside my heart and carried them without exposing them so I could deal with them. I was unaware I was heavyhearted despite my new life with Graham in America being filled with love and enjoyment.

It took me a long time to realize why I felt guilty because I did not recognize the pain I was carrying after my divorce. I did not know I should have dealt with my grief to fully be in my new relationship. I had to investigate the reason for the heaviness in my heart and let myself feel the pain. Oh, how foolish I was to neglect the wound in my heart, thinking everything was fine!

What I have realized over the years is I still grieve Graham's death and that is okay. What is not right is to hide it and pretend it is not there. Hiding grief will cast shadows on your life and heaviness in your heart. Whatever feelings you have about your loss, listen to your heart, look for where the feelings come from, and never push them away. That is the only way to heal from the pain of loss. Your heart needs your tender care.

You will notice as soon as you start paying attention to what is going on in your heart that sometimes there are multiple layers, and you may see only what you are capable of seeing at that time, so you need patience. During the process of revealing, you gain power as your heart gets lighter and you get stronger. Remember, patience and tenderness are the key to healing, and they are the opposite of being harsh with yourself.

HAVING A HEART LIGHTER THAN THE FEATHER OF TRUTH

Egyptian mythology describes what happens when a person passes on to the afterlife. The person's heart is weighted against the feather of truth, and it must be lighter for the soul to move on to the afterlife—the Field of Reeds.

I love this belief, and it is the message I want to remember for myself. I think it is good for you, too, to think about the meaning of the message and reflect on how heavy your heart is right now.

To understand what is true is not that important. What matters is your will and your intention to go on the path of finding the truth. In your spiritual journey along the path, your heart gets lighter, you feel more empowered, and your path gets clearer and more focused every day. You just need to be there and enjoy every step.

Below are five things you can do to cope with your own grief, either from the loss of a spouse, family member, or friend, or during separation from your loved ones or your lifestyle.

1. **Get enough rest:** Since we all live in modern times with busy lifestyles, you should intentionally make time to rest. Have a cup of coffee/tea and enjoy it. Go for a little walk and breathe deeply. Get a great night's sleep every night. Sleep is like a little death. While you are asleep, some part of your spirit can leave your body and communicate with other spirits to help you gain insights from different dimensions—that is one of the reasons sleep is so important.

2. **Take a vacation and spend time with yourself:** Plan your vacation for the most relaxation and be who you are. Perhaps you want to avoid noisy places, shopping, and big parties with strangers, which may stimulate and excite you but not help you relax. It is better to get away from the materialistic world and expose yourself to encountering something awesome. Do not feel guilty because you are not working and you are spending money while you are on vacation. Think of it as putting golden coins into your savings account in the universe—you will get it back with great interest in the future.

3. **Shed tears as often and as much as you want in a safe environment:** Do not hold in your emotions, especially when you are by yourself. Tears are a cleansing agent. You may feel like watching a film or listening to some music and just letting your emotions run free sometimes.

4. **Journal your thoughts:** By writing down your thoughts, they become clearer. If you can see what you are thinking, you can grasp the clue you need to heal, and sometimes seeing is enough. Your thoughts get more organized by verbalizing, and thinking logically helps you to be more grounded. This process will give you a solid foundation to grow spiritually.

5. **Talk to someone you can trust:** Whether it be a close friend, a counselor, or a support group, it is good to have someone to talk to no matter how negative your feelings might be. Find a good listener. Knowing your feelings matter and your feelings and thoughts are

heard, no matter how personal or insignificant they seem, will make you feel lighter and brighter. The power of help is more than you think, and you are so worthy of receiving help.

EXERCISE

1. Keep a pen and notebook on your bedside table and write down your first thought when you get up in the morning. If you remember your dreams, write them down in as much detail as you can. If you see certain colors, numbers, scenery, transportation, animals, foods, etc., you may find looking up the meanings in a dream dictionary interesting—you can find quite a few resources on the internet. On the lines below, write down some things you saw in your dream, the meaning you found in a dream dictionary, and your interpretation and thoughts about the dream and its meaning.

____

____

____

____

____

____

____

____

2. Write down where you will go on vacation and when. It is okay if it cannot happen right away due to your circumstances, such as work and family obligations. The point is to make a plan and stick with it. Once you plan the vacation, think about it every day and free yourself to imagine you are there. As you put more positive thoughts into it, a more solid plan and good feelings will follow. It is your reward, and you totally deserve it.

____

____

____

____

____

____

____

____

3. Set up a movie or music night for yourself. Write down the title of the movie/music you would like to set up the next time you are free. If you have the movie/music night at your place, dim the lights and light some candles. If you have some aromatic oil, that would be great to use while you watch the movie or listen to the music. Certain scents, such as frankincense, help you relax your nervous system and release

stress. You may want to prepare a cup of non-caffeinated tea and your favorite snack to enjoy the time by yourself fully.

____

____

____

____

____

____

4. On the next full or new moon, write down whatever thoughts come to mind. They can be just words, random thoughts. It is good to let your thoughts out of your mind, and by doing so intentionally, you may find some surprises in your mind you would have not realized otherwise. Those are treasures because thoughts, once out from your mind, show you how to navigate going forward.

____

____

____

____

____

____

5. Think of someone you can trust to be a good listener. Write down the name or names of people you think are trustworthy. Keep in mind that everyone has their own schedule and life. It might be more efficient to meet with a professional counselor for help with your grief because your grief is specific to you and specialists have more knowledge and experience. They are willing to help you since that is why they chose their profession. Use the lines below to write down information about the professional you found through someone you trust.

____

____

____

____

____

____

SUMMARY

My intention in writing this chapter was to shine a light on the place deep in my mind where I was hiding grief. I had been unable to dig into this space because I was afraid. I was afraid of an unknown field of my own psyche as if a huge monster named Negativity was hidden in there. Over the years, the unseen part was weighing down my heart. I knew I had to reveal it, and now was the right time to do it. I had been preparing for this time, and I finally conjured up the courage and power to pull the monster out. Once I put it under the light, just like in *The Wizard of Oz* when Dorothy throws a bucket of water on the Wicked Witch, it melted away—the negativity melted and was purged and something different appeared.

The last words Graham said to me, with tears in his eyes, were, "Thank you for finding me." This refrain still rings in my ears today. I remember those words and the surrounding scenery in the background when he said it. I thought they were beautiful words; however, their meaning did not really sink into my heart. I was unable to receive them as his sincere gratitude toward me because I thought I did not deserve his sincerity, his gratitude, and his love for me because my heart was not fully with him.

Now, as I am able to look back and reveal and accept my negative feelings, they have transformed into a new form of love. I am fully honored to have loved and been loved in this lifetime with him, and I salute my journey. I hope you, too, can live this same way: feel the pain, work through your grief, release your pain, heal, and love again.

Chapter 9

Gaining Self-Confidence

"The most common way people give up their power
is by thinking they don't have any."

— Alice Walker

If you experience the loss of love by either separation or death, going through pain is inevitable as we talked about in the last chapter. Your heart is broken, and you lament for who knows how long. Sometimes when you encounter tremendous difficulty, you freeze and numb yourself to avoid feeling because it is too painful to bear. It is like being anesthetized when you undergo a serious operation—you numb the feelings in your heart for a while. After the operation, you must wake up from anesthesia just as your feelings will have to be woken up. Setting yourself free from the frozen chain of fear, you feel again, and your heart starts beating strong and singing a song of love again.

In this chapter, I want to talk about self-confidence because it is the best way to set yourself free from the heavy chains of a difficult situation and regain your power to stand.

BELIEVE IN YOUR INNER STRENGTH

You may have heard that challenges are there for you to overcome and become stronger. When you are in a difficult situation, it may be hard to think that way. When I am dealing with challenging matters, I, too, sometimes feel it is almost too difficult to break through them.

When I was going through the most challenging days in my life as Graham became weaker every day, one of my friends said, "Think of yourself as a tree. In a storm, the tree is blown by violent winds and severely hit by horrendous rain. Branches are bent and some leaves are blown off, but the tree remains standing. The roots under the ground support the tree above the ground, and the tree does not break. It is just waiting for the storm to pass, and when it passes, the tree once again spreads its branches and leaves, and blossoms when spring comes."

My friend's words of encouragement helped me remain grounded and kept my soul from being defeated during a time of tremendous difficulty. I still remember his words, and whenever I feel I am in a storm, I believe in myself and my strength. I think of myself as a tree with roots. My roots are my strength, which I was born with, and they connect me to other spirits, including my ancestors, guardian angels, and the Universe or higher beings, whatever you wish to call them. They are my roots, and I am with them and supported by them. By believing in their existence and my own strength, I can stand strong no matter what situation I face.

PRACTICING MEDITATION

I like to sit quietly and meditate. I have practiced different meditation techniques, including vipassana, which is sitting for ten days without talking to nor making eye contact with anyone. As you sit quietly with your eyes and mouth shut, you become so in tune with your senses. You become observant of yourself—you hear your breath, feel your heartbeat, and sense your energy vibrating. The vipassana meditation method I learned was to clear your mind and maintain the clearness to wish for peace. Many methods of meditation exist, and what you aim to gain through meditation might be different depending on your circumstances. The point of meditation, in my opinion, is to train yourself to get in touch with yourself and see the beauty within you.

Meditation lets you look inside your soul, and when you sense your soul as a vibrant being, you gain the ability to believe in your own beauty and strength. You are much more than what you possess in materials or in your outer appearance. I find meditation is a great practice for gaining self-confidence.

LOGIC HELPS TO FREE YOURSELF AND OTHERS

Zora Neale Hurston was an American author who lived from 1891 to 1960. In her work, she portrayed the lives and struggles of African Americans in the South. In her prime, she was a successful and significant Black writer. Over a thirty-year career, she published fifty-some pieces, including novels, folklore, an autobiography, short stories, essays, articles, and plays.

Hurston intensively researched African-American and Caribbean folklore. Her book *Mules and Men* written in 1935 is a collection of African-American folklore based on her anthropological and folkloric fieldwork. She also commented on the sexual slavery perpetrated on Black women by white men.

Hurston is described as a pioneer of Black women's empowerment because of her numerous works based on her study of her anthropological origins and her strong belief that Black women could be independent and powerful.

However, Hurston met criticism for opposing integration, which she did not see as the solution to solve discrimination against African Americans. She was also criticized for her representation of voodoo and being vague about racial politics and Black feminism. Despite producing masterful works, she received very little financial reward. The most she ever earned in royalties from any of her books was $943.75, according to the Zora Neale Hurston official website.

Hurston had a stroke and died of hypertensive heart disease at St. Lucie County Welfare Home. After her death in 1960, the man who was told to clean her house was burning her papers when Officer Patrick DuVal passed by and put out the fire, saving much of her work. Her novels were forgotten by the literary world for years until 1975, when

Alice Walker (Pulitzer Prize winning author of *The Color Purple*) reintroduced Hurston's genius work.

Zora Neale Hurston said, "I have the nerve to walk my own way, however hard, in my search for reality, rather than climb upon the rattling wagon of wishful illusions."

Through her search for truth, Hurston never gave up her pride as a Black woman, and she blazed a trail for the next generation—setting an example of pride, freedom, and independence for future generations.

Alice Walker said, "But it is crucial for Black women to hold on to this very special tradition that we have…where you free yourself and you go back and you free other people." I see Walker's confidence as one who achieved great success, freedom, and independence through her work and studies, and as a successor of her fellow Black female author, Hurston, she helped to continue Hurston's legacy as a role model for future generations.

DEVELOPING DETERMINATION AND PATIENCE

I admire people who have gone through challenges and see value in them, knowing it is worth their effort to overcome them. By making the effort with determination and patience, they gain unshakable confidence.

I have a friend who was an Olympic skier. To become a world class, top athlete, she trained from a very early age and cultivated her skills and concentration. After she retired from skiing, she started her new carrier as a neurokinetic therapist and trainer to help other people. She then shifted her passion from competitive skiing to helping and supporting others. She learned to lead with confidence from the experience she had gained through her training and determination in becoming an Olympian.

Another friend went to the Himalayas when he was in his mid-twenties. His major in college was environmental studies, and he was hired by a resort development company when he graduated. He told me when he got the job, he wanted to see how developers approached environmental issues, so he was determined to stay at the company for at least two years. He worked at a resort hotel and soon saw how poorly the corporation managed its effect on the environment and nature. He and his coworkers decided to separate all the recyclables that had been thrown in with the trash. He quit the job when the recycling process was complete. He had seen enough.

After quitting, my friend went to the Himalayas to climb mountains. It took him two months to reach the base camp of Mount Everest on foot, and from there, he climbed to the summit of Island Peak at 20,226 feet.

He told me, "It was a team effort to reach the top of the mountain, which was covered by icy snow. We were all from different countries, different backgrounds and cultures, but we developed a great friendship." He added, "I did not bend my beliefs about protecting the environment in the face of corporate policy, and then I made my dream to climb a mountain in the Himalayas come true and met wonderful people. The feelings of achievement gave me confidence that has been supporting me ever since.

To this day, he works for sustainability, to protect the environment, and to help us humans coexist with nature.

KNOWING HOW POWERFUL YOU ARE

You are a powerful being, as we all are. The key to embracing and harnessing your power is to know you possess it. If you are in a difficult situation due to your culture, politics, gender, relationships, finances, or health, do not give up. Keep on believing in yourself and your power. Know that the positive thoughts themselves are the most powerful prayer you can offer yourself. Knowing you have the power gives you confidence, and that helps you break through challenges. Here are five tips for realizing your own power and gaining confidence.

1. **Feel your soul and its connection to the center of the earth:** The first thing I do when I sit for meditation is close my eyes, feel my breath, and focus on my core and its connection to Mother Earth's core. I recommend trying to imagine there is a cord connecting you from your buttocks through the ground all the way to the earth's core. The cord is very strong and big so you can safely drain any unwanted thoughts, feeling, and/or emotions you have been carrying through it. Once they reach the core of the earth, they are cleansed by the earth and returned to the universe. It is not your job to cleanse them. You just let the earth and universe take them and purify them for the good. Then you can focus on yourself.

2. **Knowledge is your armor:** I have seen some people focus on their spiritual growth and let their logic slip. The result is they tend to lack the understanding to support their own ideas, will, and determination, and they rely on guidance from others too much. Some view that kind of psyche in Jungian terms as "a mood of friendly weakness." You can learn from others with experience and knowledge, but you do not have to follow their beliefs as if they were your own. You have the ability to study, gain knowledge, and learn. It is totally up to you to choose if you will use the knowledge and develop it to add to your own wisdom.

3. **Do not wait for approval or applause:** It is natural to desire recognition. In fact, social theories have described it as a vital human need. The point is to avoid waiting for it because it is a distraction, making it difficult to stay focused and centered. You will realize as you focus on your own achievements that people around you will naturally recognize you and treat you with more respect and admiration. You will meet new people who are more interesting and attractive as you gain confidence because you shine with a different aura.

4. **Help and support others in need:** Helping others helps you feel good about yourself. Giving help is equally as important as receiving help. Look at it like parents becoming mature adults by raising children who need constant help and support from the moment they are born. It is a wonderful feeling when you observe a child's growth. Your heart gets filled with satisfaction and you know what you did was right.

5. **Be grateful and humble:** As you achieve your goals, you will see clearly you are not standing alone. Where you are today is based on what others have done before you, for you, and with you. They may not be close to you or around you now. They may be pets or your natural surroundings, or they may be people you have interacted with in the past. Nothing happens by accident. It is a natural law that you are given more if you are humble and appreciative.

EXERCISE

1. Set a piece of paper and colored pencils or pens in front of you. Sit with your back straight on a comfortable chair, put your hands on your lap naturally, put the tip of your tongue at the back of your upper front teeth, and exhale and inhale deeply several times. Now close your eyes and imagine a cord as wide as your buttocks going down all the way to the center of the earth. When you feel it reach the core of the earth, visualize what color it and your aura are. There is no right or wrong, and the color may be different from day to day. Draw what you visualized in color on the piece of paper.

2. What kinds of things are you interested in? Maybe you are interested in family history, religion, the myths of your country, arts, health, your partner, pets, etc. I recommend studying the origin of the particular thing or person you are curious about in depth. The process of studying, rather than what you find, is the important part. The knowledge you gain becomes your confidence and strength. Write down what you want to study about and its key words in the lines below.

____

____

____

____

____

3. How can you start studying the thing or person you listed in question two? Depending on the subject, you can call a family member or your partner and ask specific questions. You can go to the library, look for information on the internet, or go to seminars or lectures. Write down the actions you will take to learn about the thing or person you want to find out more about.

____

____

____

____

____

____

4. Once you start studying, plan to stick to it. Set a time aside for studying at your own pace. It is best to continue studying while you still remember what you learned, so I recommend doing it at

least once a week. Determination is important here. Set up your study time for the next four weeks and write the schedule below. When you have completed each study session, check off each block of time you had scheduled.

____

____

____

____

____

5. During your research, who and what did you find you are grateful for learning more about? Write down five things or people whose importance you had not realized or not paid attention to before you started studying.

____

____

____

____

____

____

SUMMARY

Self-confidence has been studied for its effects on happiness and success for years, and many tips for gaining self-confidence have been suggested in various articles. In this chapter, I wanted to share what worked for me in cultivating self-confidence over the years. You can attain a strong will, your wishes for yourself, and your desire to help others by having faith in yourself, a clear mind, logical thinking, determination, and gratitude.

Chapter 10

Loving Yourself

"If you don't love yourself, nobody will.
Not only that,
you won't be good at loving anyone else.
Loving starts with the self."

— Wayne Dyer

Self-confidence is something you gain by making an effort over time. It is something you get as the result of your achievements gained through will and determination. You look at and think of yourself in relation to others, either people or matters; therefore, it is the yang aspect of self-empowerment. Self-love also predominantly comes from your efforts and willpower, but it is more yin, which means you work inwardly and give rather than gain. In this chapter, let's look at what self-love is and why it is necessary on your path toward living the art of love and loving yourself.

WE ARE MADE OF STARDUST

On the island of Molokai, I once stayed at my friend's place for a week while the family was on a trip. I stayed to take care of their land and animals, including a horse, ducks, a cat, a rabbit, and a dog. It was a perfect place to enjoy my lone staycation. The day started early at sunrise when I watered the plants in the garden and fed the animals. It all went seamlessly—I prepared meals for myself and the cat and dog, swam in the homemade swimming pool in the yard, picked mangos, watched orange turn to pink and purple in the sky from the deck at sunset, and went to bed with a little dachshund crawling into bed with me.

It was so quiet at night that I could feel it was time for everyone, including animals, to sleep and go freely into the dream world—a world in which your astral body travels and has experiences different from when you are awake. That night, the little dachshund woke me up—he wanted to go outside for a pee. I got up, still half asleep, and opened the sliding door for him. He rushed out. I just followed him to the yard without any thoughts. Molokai is an island of only about 7,500 people. Where I was had no streetlights, so the stars over Molokai are more spectacular than over Maui. I looked up and saw a dark royal blue sky studded with millions of brightly shining stars. The Milky Way was running like a sparkly river, and even though I do not have much knowledge about constellations, I recognized Cygnus, the swan.

I was stunned by its beauty. I do not know how long I stood there looking up. In the next moment, I was eye to eye with the dachshund, and I felt as if he were saying, "See. Now you get it." I was alone in the middle of the night in someone's yard, no one but the little dachshund sitting next to me, across the sea from my home—I knew no one and had no one to talk to on the island, but my heart was full.

In that moment, I understood happiness is in the moment, yet it is eternal. At the same time, deep in my soul, I remembered in looking at the sky that I was looking at my home—we are made of stardust. The feeling was so comforting. We are made of love, and we have nothing to lose, nothing is missing from us, and there is nothing to be afraid of.

THE ART OF LISTENING

In his book *Man for Himself: An Inquiry into the Psychology of Ethics*, written in 1947, Jewish German-American psychologist and sociologist Erich Fromm wrote, "Not only others, but we ourselves are the 'object' of our feelings and attitudes; the attitudes toward others and toward ourselves, far from being contradictory, are basically conjunctive."

He also wrote, "Love of others and love of ourselves are not alternatives." I could not agree more that it is essential to give love to yourself the same as you give love to others. Moreover, I think your ability to love others is dependent on loving yourself.

Loving yourself and being a selfish, egoistic person are different. In *The Art of Listening*, Fromm wrote:

> In the philosophic tradition you find it very clear that narcissism or Ego-centricity is something entirely different from self-love. Because self-love is love, and in love it doesn't make any difference who the object of my love is. I am a human being

myself. Man must have an affirmative, loving attitude towards oneself.

His word "affirmative" implies you need a positive, supportive, and encouraging attitude toward yourself. He continues, "The egocentric person in reality is a person who does not love himself, and so he is greedy. In general, a greedy person is a person who is not satisfied." In other words, a self-loving person is satisfied with themselves and has positive feelings and attitudes toward themselves.

The question is, how can you be satisfied with and positive and supportive of yourself?

Fromm said listening is a key art in being satisfied, and particularly, he likened it to the art of understanding poetry. He then provided six basic rules for this art that include concentration as a listener, freedom from anxiety and greed, a free-working imagination that can express itself in words, a capacity for empathy, the strength to feel others' experiences as if they were your own, and the ability to understand another's love language/needs.

Fromm said, "Understanding and loving are inseparable. If they are separate, it is a cerebral process and the door to essential understanding remains closed." He is saying listening is the art of understanding, which is necessary for loving.

What does Fromm mean by listening is an art like understanding poetry? When you think of poetry, does a particular poem come to mind? If so, why do you think you remember it over others? What do you like about the poem? How do you immerse yourself in the world of the poem?

Your inner world is rich like your favorite poem, full of feelings and characters, colors and seasons, and words that can represent so much. Go play in your own poetry, which is your inner world, as if you were an enthusiastic child.

When you are satisfied you've stayed there long enough, come back. You have to come back. My hula teacher told me hula means dance between heaven and earth. Life is a dance. You can dance between your heaven, in your inner world, and earth, your outer world, and most importantly, enjoy your dance and have fun dancing in both inner and outer worlds back and forth.

GIVE YOURSELF A TRIP

After you have done something major, or whenever you feel a calling, it is great to take a trip and spend time on yourself. Choose whether to go by yourself or with friends or your partner, the destination, accommodations, and how long you will be gone. Traveling starts the moment you decide to go, and you should enjoy planning, which is the beginning of your trip.

I just came back from a short trip to Amanohashidate, which translates as "heaven's bridge." It is one of the Three Views of Japan, the canonical list of Japan's three most celebrated scenic sights. I decided to go on the trip after I finished writing the eighth chapter of this book, the one about coping with grief. It was a significant process for me, and I wanted some reflection and rejuvenation time for myself.

I have spent more time overseas than in Japan since I moved away in my early twenties, and now, I want to see more of my native country. I would like to explore many places, but this time I was drawn to this particular place, Amanohashidate, which is located north of Kyoto by the Sea of Japan. It is part of the island of Japan's creation myth.

A strip of land connects two opposing sides of the bay. The strip is narrow, 2.1 miles, and is covered with about 7,000 pine trees. The Sea of Japan has a different atmosphere from the Pacific Ocean, which I am well accustomed to, living in the Bay Area in California and in Hawaii.

I crossed the strip by bicycle to visit the shrine on the other side of the bay from where I stayed. While I was pedaling, I felt the sun shining through the pine branches while a gentle breeze and many singing birds gave me a peaceful feeling. I took a lift up the hill to see the scenic view of the bay. The contrast of the hill's green and the blue sea was breathtakingly beautiful. The shrine was on top of the hill surrounded by a bamboo forest. It is not a well-advertised attraction, so there are few visitors, which I am thankful for because it helps to keep it serene.

The site features a giant tree, which has been worshiped since ancient times because the spirits of creation goddesses and gods of reside there. I bowed, put my palms together, and prayed for peace and health.

The hotel has onsen (a hot spring and bathing), and I enjoyed the warm earth and water energy as it refreshed and rejuvenated me. On the first night, I read poetry, *Midaregami* (Tangled Hair) written by my favorite poet, Akiko Yosano. On the second day, I went to a museum to see art created by a female Japanese copperplate painter for poems written by Spanish poet Juan Ramón Jiménez, who won the Nobel Prize for literature. The title of the collection is *Platero and I. Midaregami* and *Platero and I* have very different styles, but they are both full of emotion. *Midaregami* is about Yosano's passionate love for her husband to be, as you can see in her famous poem below:

> *"yawa hada no atsuki chishio ni fure mo mi de sabishikarazuya michi o toku kimi"*

> "Not even once have you touched my soft flesh, coursing hot blood. Don't you feel a bit lonesome, you always preaching your way?"

Platero and I is about Jiménez while he was recovering from a mental breakdown. With his loyal donkey Platero, Jiménez sees tenderness, innocence, and the simple joys of life. The scenes, including the excerpt below, are depicted by the copper painter, Yoko Yamamoto, and each etching gives visual images to *Platero and I* as if the poetry written 100 years ago has received new life.

> Do not worry, Platero, for I shall bury you at the foot of the tall round pine in the orchard at the Piña, which you like so much. You will be close to life's serenity and mirth. The children will

play around you and the girls will sew in their tiny low chairs at your side. You will know the verses which loneliness will bring me.

I did not expect to encounter those two poetry collections by different writers during my trip, but they came to me and showed me their passion, which resonated with me, inspiring me. I gratefully accepted the gifts from nature, spirits of the land, and art created by fellow humans on this trip. It was well worth the time and money I spent for my solo trip. I know my journey continues, and life is preparing many more opportunities for me to encounter beauty in various aspects if I keep opening my eyes and my heart. It is so for you too.

WALKING EACH OTHER HOME

As Ram Dass, a former resident of Maui and famous spiritual leader who recently passed, often said, "We are all just walking each other home." That was a favorite quote of Sarah, one of my best friends who passed away in 2021 at the age of forty-nine. When she was diagnosed with a terminal illness a year and half prior to her death, she did not fear death. In fact, she was happy to share her gratitude for her life, husband, family, and friends, and she said she got a golden ticket to reincarnation. She was happy because she knew she was going home to heaven with everyone's love for her and her love to everyone walking her home. I would like to emphasize you are walking yourself home along with other spirits. You should be nice to yourself first so you can be nice to others. I've listed five things you can do in your daily life to remember that the principle of loving starts within.

1. **Be positive when you speak:** Words and sounds are so powerful. In my opinion, your power as a human is being able to use verbalized words to influence others and the world around you. You can change situations around you using words. So, it is always wise to choose what you say carefully. When you make wishes, always state them in a positive way. I have a friend who told me before she met her husband that she was praying to meet someone who was not fat. It turned out the guy she met and married is a little bit overweight. She was laughing when she said, "I should have wished to meet a lean guy, instead of not fat. I made a mistake using negative words." Training yourself to say positive things will affect your way of thinking and attitude. You will soon start noticing the difference in your mindset, the way situations turn out, and the way people around you treat you when you express your thoughts in a positive way.

2. **It is okay to ask for help:** When you are in trouble, you can get help. People can help you if you let them. Most importantly, you need to believe in the divine's love and power to empower you and people around you who may be messengers from the divine.

3. **Be active for yourself:** If you want to know love, you have to go deep inside your heart. Love comes not only through compassion but also by being empathetic. Empathy allows you to connect to another's essence. It also requires introspection, which allows you to connect with your own essence. The difference between love and all other emotions is love involves active and continuous effort and willpower while other emotions are passive and transient,

springing up within based on your thoughts, others, and your surroundings. Know that self-love cannot be achieved passively, and make an active effort to love yourself.

4. **Make yourself feel good:** Surround yourself with beautiful things that make you feel relaxed and nice. Wear comfortable clothes that make you feel beautiful and sensual. Do not feel guilty about acquiring things for yourself if they improve the quality of your life and your feelings. You may choose things purely for your pleasure, which is different from buying things to get approval or admiration from others.

5. **Invest more time and money in travel:** When you travel, you meet new friends here and there, you experience new cultures, and you develop more gratitude and get a new perspective on life. You may find a new place to live. Traveling can open up new possibilities and show you new directions for your future.

EXERCISE

1. Write down five nice things about yourself below. You can be specific. Include your name, for example, "Anne, the wrinkles around your eyes are giving you special charms as you mature," or "Michael, you called your sister, who just lost her dog. It is very caring of you." Continue doing this every day for a week, and you will see a difference in how you think about yourself.

    ____

    ____

    ____

    ____

    ____

2. Take two small pieces of paper. Write "You are beautiful" and "I love you" on each piece and stick them to the mirror you look at most often. You may want to use a colorful pen and paper to be decorative. Write as if you are writing a little love note to yourself. After you stick those two pieces of paper to your mirror, look at them every day. Then write down how you feel different. You may want to add more paper with your own words. Below, write down other things you want to say to yourself to give love.

    ____

    ____

    ____

3. Get a doll or a stuffed animal for yourself. It is your inner child. Have the doll around you at home; perhaps sleep with it. Talk to it as if you are talking to yourself as a child. Look at it tenderly, hug it gently, and be nice to the doll. By doing so, you will be healing your deep trauma, which you got early in life. You may not remember the feelings of being hurt specifically, but you may still have some aches in your heart, and it is nice to give healing energy to your inner child through your doll. Write down what kind of doll or stuffed animal you want to get for yourself. I got a mermaid with pink hair and turquoise-blue tail with hidden legs inside the tail.

    ____

    ____

    ____

4. Go star gazing. Stars can tell you many things. In *The Little Prince* by Antoine de Saint-Exupéry is this quote about stars: "All men have stars, but they are not the same things for different people. For some, who are travelers, the stars are guides. For others they are no more than little lights in the sky. For others, who are scholars, they are problems.... But all these stars are silent. You—you alone—will have stars as no one else has them." Which stars do you have?

    ____

    ____

    ____

5. Buy new clothes or lingerie that make you feel comfortable and good. You may want to choose silk, especially for lingerie, because its smooth texture and shiny glow will make you feel special and flamboyant. It is a gift for yourself, and you do not need an excuse to treat yourself nicely. Enjoy shopping for yourself for no special occasion.

SUMMARY

Love starts within. To love and be loved, you must love yourself first. Because love is the emotion that involves active and continuous effort and willpower, you need to train yourself to actively pursue love. In other words, love can be attained if you are determined and if you believe in yourself. Always listen to what your heart tells you first. Meditation is great because it gives you quiet time to reflect on your thoughts. Remember, you are like a poem, so enjoy reading. You can develop your inner richness through self-love, the richness of millions of stars in the sky.

Chapter 11

Loving Fully

"The love you withhold is the pain that you
carry lifetime after lifetime."

— Alex Collier

Loving yourself is the most important part in the art of love, which is a lifelong practice. How you love others is a reflection of how you love yourself. Self-love is completely opposite to selfishness and narcissism, which comes from being unsatisfied. If you want to love fully, you must love yourself fully. In this chapter, let's look at what "to love fully" means.

WHAT IS LOVE?

Have you asked yourself, "What is love?" Have you talked about what love is with your partner and your children?

I have asked a group of my friends this question. Interestingly, the answers varied from person to person, and everyone's answer was unique and matched their character. These are the key words mentioned by my friends: aloha, trees in the forest, snow over the mountain, waves, mother's instinct, every cell of my body, flower petals, flowers that bloom in the heart, birds, relationships with everything that exists, the true us as humans, generations to come, teachers, elders, peace, hope, grace, the universe, warmth, ancestors, human voices, nighttime sky, darkness, stars, all the children in the world, circle, sun, moon, art, music, soil, raindrops, little things, earth, parents, sky, green, clouds, heart, breath, miracles, vibrations, intuition, empathy, pets, all the emotions, to take actions, sea, bubbles of the sea, something that is always there, trust without anxiety, light lit in the heart, including the light of kindness, light of warmth, light of hope, and light of prayer.

One of my friends said even anger is love. I totally agree with him, and moreover, I define the opposite of love as no feelings and no interest, which differs from hatred or anger. When you lose the feelings of love, your feelings do not move, and you do not have emotions toward the objects, whether they are a certain person or a thing.

HAVING THE HEART IN

In Western culture, we tend to prioritize being logical over being emotional. That is because we value monetized productivity. I am not saying being productive to make money is a problem. It has just been overprioritized, and it seems that tendency continues.

I have studied at the Happiness Lab, which is a course at Yale University focused on providing knowledge about positive psychology and new evidence-based discoveries supporting the need for building individual wellbeing. It is the most popular class in Yale's 300-year history. One of the most interesting studies I learned about measured one's happiness in relation to how much money they have. It showed money to a certain amount does contribute to one's happiness. You can easily imagine you need some money to buy things to live comfortably and feel free. However, the study shows that beyond a certain amount, more money does not make you happier. The study also measured one's wellbeing by comparing the level of positive emotions before and after buying a new car. The level goes up higher when the person gets a new car, but that boost in happiness lasts only about two weeks.

On the contrary, what makes happiness last is when people are engaged in something and in the state of flow, feeling loved and supported, having a sense of purpose and being healthy. The PERMA-Profiler is an assessment defined by Dr. Martin E. P. Seligman in his book *Flourish*, published in 2011, as the five pillars of well-being:

- Positive emotion
- Engagement
- Relationship
- Meaning
- Accomplishment

Positive emotions are the good feelings you have about your current situation and state of being, and they are also hopeful and optimistic feelings that encourage you to feel good about the future. Engagement refers to the degree of attention, interest, curiosity, and passion you have when you are doing something, and if you have high degrees of those, you are well engaged. Relationships refer to feeling supported, loved, and valued by other people. Meaning is a continuous engagement in purpose that drives you to live and be one with the higher calling throughout life. Accomplishment is defined as achievement, mastery, or competence, and a sense of accomplishment is a result of working toward goals and being self-motivated to finish what you set out to do.

The PERMA-Profiler measures these five pillars, along with negative emotion and health. You can find the assessment online at https://www.authentichappiness.sas.upenn.edu/. You may find it interesting to take it from time to time to measure your level of well-being.

All five pillars of PERMA are governed by your heart rather than your brain. None of PERMA can be achieved without passion, which is the fire burning in your heart, not in your head, although the brain can help you understand the meaning and the reason you feel how you feel, which makes it easier to be assured of your own emotions.

Emotions, even negative ones, tell us a lot. Irritation, cynicism, and exhaustion are often signs of being burnt out. When you recognize the signs of negative emotions, using your logical analyzation skills, you can prevent yourself from damaging your career, relationships, and health. Thus, you can develop your positive judging skills to understand what is going on in your heart, and that becomes wisdom rather than mere knowledge.

GIVING AND RECEIVING HELP

When you numb your feelings to avoid pain, your heart gets rigid because you tighten it to protect it from possible harm from outside. It is important to have boundaries, yet you can still be open to receiving help from others when you need it.

As I write this in 2023, we are still feeling the effects of the global pandemic. We do not feel the same. Our society is more fearful, and we feel uncertain.

Many people were isolated during the height of the pandemic, leaving them feeling lonely and dejected. You may know elderly people who live alone who felt more and more isolated over the first three years. People are meant to have close social interactions, so the limitations during the pandemic made us, especially the elderly, feel anxious and weaker. It has been difficult to say the least to ask for and get help. This is a difficult situation for both people who need help and people who wish to help because it is human nature to help. We are meant to help each other. Cutting off interactions is like taking away our hope.

The song "You've Got a Friend" by Carole King was written in 1971. King told *Mojo Magazine*, "The song was as close to pure inspiration as I've ever experienced. The song wrote itself. It was written by something outside myself, through me."

When the song was written, America was at war in Vietnam. I have a friend who was sent to Vietnam at nineteen against his will. He had protested the war as a "flower child" in San Francisco. He had his twentieth birthday on the battlefield. He told me, "I remember thinking, *Oh great, people are shooting at me on my birthday.*"

After two weeks on the battlefield, his entire platoon was wiped out. He was the only survivor because he appeared to be dead. Then he put his dog tag on the body of another soldier who was unrecognizable so the military would think he was dead. This gave him time to escape to Hawaii. In a valley with a deep jungle covered by lush greens and hundreds of kinds of flowers on the island of Kauai, he lived with a small group of people and waited for the war to end.

He lives on Maui now. I met him when he gave me an astrology reading. He is an astonishing astrologer, and for fifty years, he has helped so many people with his readings. He often tells me he needs to do something to help others; otherwise, he cannot feel purpose and meaning in his life. He said, "I am losing my hope by observing what is going on in the world nowadays. People used to be nicer to each other, and we helped and supported each other before, but that seems less and less true now."

We must remember our true value and that the meaning of life is always to support each other, to grow to be better humans, and to actively act upon kindness and care. Remember, we are receiving at the same time we are giving. We and others, whether it be other people, animals, plants, or any objects, are all related and interconnected beyond time. Energy is always circulating—going out and coming in, giving and receiving. I still want to believe in our goodness as humans, and I do not give up because it is our responsibility and mission to leave this planet better for future generations than we found it, and that gives me a strong sense of purpose. I put out my vibration of hope and belief, and I receive help and support from the Universe without knowing when and in what form, but I am certain I will be honored to receive when it is given to me as my rewards for loving myself and loving life.

DAWN IN DARKNESS

In ancient Hawaii, people believed the day began when the sun set, and this was the time to make a wish for the new day. Long ago, people from Tahiti came to Hawaii by canoe. They paddled at night because they used the stars to guide them. If you are surrounded by nothing but a vast sea, especially at night in the dark, you can only look up for the light of stars and the moon.

In *Rig Veda*, a verbal folk story of the ancient Hindu, the goddess of light and the goddess of darkness are both worshiped. We need darkness to see the light.

We live as if we are on a long voyage surrounded by a vast ocean and the dark of night. We may encounter shark attacks if we are not careful and prepared. However hard, we should keep our chins up, look up, and use our wisdom to get directions from stars and make wishes for a safe journey to the new land. In the extremes, we feel we can only rely on love—love for ourselves, for others, of others, for the unknown, and of the unknown.

Below are five things I do daily to love fully. You can practice the same habits, attain well-being, and make the world a better place. If we all follow these practices, I believe we can really change the world, one by one, little by little, and believe it or not, it is already happening.

1. **Love wholeheartedly:** When you love someone, that is your best opportunity to grow. Love as much as you can and try even beyond your capacity and capability. Focus on cultivating inner wisdom, which is love, instead of seeking stimulation from outside. You learn so much by trying to understand the person you love. Think of the person you love as your mirror reflection, and realize you look into your heart by looking into their heart. You understand yourself and your needs at the same time as you understand your loved one. If you want to grow, do not restrain your love. Love is abundant, infinite, and eternal. Nothing can provide more life lessons, joy, and growth than loving someone.

2. **Put full effort into understanding:** Understanding is essential for love. Its importance is more in the effort of understanding than whether you logically understand in your brain. Listen to what others say; read their body language, tone of voice, and facial expressions; and pay attention to all the subtleties in the atmosphere when you are with someone, and even in texts. Read between the lines, and constantly and immediately ask if you are not certain of what they mean and confirm what you think you heard/understand is correct.

3. **Prioritize your loved ones:** Always ensure your loved ones feel like your top priority. Nothing is more valuable than the people you love and who love you. Think of your loved ones, especially your partner, as those you interacted with in your previous lives and perhaps in

your next. As we are all walking each other home, we are traveling through lifetimes with other souls, and the person you have the closest relationship with is often your soulmate. Your relationship with them may last a very long time or may end relatively quickly, but no matter how long it lasts, you have some lessons to learn and master through the relationship with that particular person to get to the next step in your soul's journey.

4. **Spend as much time as you can communicating with your partner:** To understand one another, you must put sincere effort into communicating. I want to emphasize that understanding starts within. Be sincere with yourself first, spend time with yourself, and listen carefully to what your inner voice tells you. It is important to hold yourself in your heart firmly and feel its warmth. By doing so, you establish an unshakable belief in yourself, which is your inner strength. Use your strong and warm heart to communicate with your partner through your heart space.

5. **Be an example to your children of what loving fully does for you and the family:** Children are fast learners because they have pure hearts and absorb what they see. Even if you do not tell them directly, they can sense what is going on and how you are feeling. Remember, if you love wholeheartedly, you start the movement and circulation of love between the person you give love to and receive love from. That circulation creates a positive vibration, which spreads to your surroundings, most likely in your family first, then beyond into time and space. All you need to do is believe in the power of love.

EXERCISE

1. Call your partner often to ask how they are doing. Many use text messaging more than calling, which is fine. However, listening to each other's voice makes communication more personal and real. Make a phone call today and write down the key words from your conversation.

    ____

    ____

    ____

    ____

2. Set up a date to spend memorable and valuable time with your partner. If you are married and have children, it is important to have separate time as a couple and talk about yourselves. Plan a date once a week, biweekly, once a month at least, and choose not to talk about your children but about yourselves. Write down when, where, and how you are going to have a date with your partner.

    ____

    ____

    ____

    ____

3. Make some space and time for yourself to reflect on your feelings. People tend to focus on the other person's feelings in a relationship. Although thinking of your partner is natural, you must remember this person is a reflection of yourself. As if looking in a mirror, you can see yourself by looking at your partner. That is why you can learn so much through relationships. Your focus should be yourself, not the one you see in the mirror, and you cannot spend all day just looking in the mirror. Act on your own wishes and desires instead of reacting to another's. Have a cup of tea by yourself, listen to your favorite music, take a trip away from your partner, or do whatever makes you feel calm and lets you be yourself—now write down how you feel.

____

____

____

____

____

____

4. Make time in your life for integration and rejuvenation. Ensure you take time and prioritize relaxing and taking good care of yourself. You can set up a ritual where you take a nice long bath every night, and if you live close to water—ocean, river, waterfall, or lake—you know how good it feels to take a dip in it. Eat pure and life-filled

foods and do some gentle exercise. You can benefit so much from integration and rejuvenation because you get more energy from it. Write down what you eat for every meal for a week and reflect on your diet. You may want to adjust your eating habits accordingly.

____

____

____

____

____

____

____

5. Express your gratitude to your partner. Sounds are more powerful than you may think. Masaru Emoto showed photographs of ice crystals in his best-selling book *The Hidden Messages in Water*, claiming water is the blueprint of reality and emotional energies and vibrations can change its physical structure. You can find an image online of perfectly beautiful ice crystals of water that formed for the words "thank you." Our bodies are 60 percent water, so we can fill ourselves with positive emotions, including gratitude and love, and if we verbalize positive emotions, the energy and vibration will transmute and affect others around you directly when they hear what you say. Write down how you are grateful for your partner below and then tell them.

____

____

____

____

____

____

____

SUMMARY

We are connected with other lives, the planet, and the Universe through our roots. Especially with people whom you have close relationships, you relate to each other deeply over lifetimes. If you can feel your roots and the connection to the other person's roots, your heart will be automatically filled with great gratitude for the miracles of life. All you need to do is feel and not be afraid to love. Life is short, yet the soul is eternal. Love brings the joy of living, so love fully.

Chapter 12

Nurturing You as a Whole

"Anthropocentric as the gardener may be, he recognizes
that he is dependent for his health and survival on many
other forms of life, so he is careful to take their interests into
account in whatever he does. Wildness, he has found, resides
not only out there, but right here: in his soil, in his plants,
even in himself. The gardener cultivates wildness, but he does
so carefully and respectfully, in full recognition of its mystery."

— Michael Pollan

We are all living on the planet like the gardener who cultivates the wilderness. We are dependent for our health and survival on many other forms of life, and we nurture our soul with respect and care by recognizing its mystery.

If you live to love fully by following the path of the art of love every day, you will soon recognize the mystery of life, which is the key to nurturing your soul. Your soul knows more than your brain can understand. In this chapter, let's talk about the great benefits of nurturing yourself as a whole, which includes your body, your spirit, and your soul.

HOLISM AND SYNERGY

Vitalism theory has a long history in medical philosophies dating back to the father of medicine, the fifth-century BC Greek physician Hippocrates. He proposed in his theory that emotions have a predominantly physiological basis and differences are due specifically to fluctuations in body fluids called "humors." In Eastern tradition, a similar idea has been stated as the existence of qi or prana.

Vitalism posited that the nature of life results from a vital force peculiar to living organisms, which are fundamentally different from non-living entities. This vital force is held to control form and development and direct the organism's activities. Living entities contain some fluid, or a distinctive spirit, which is often referred to as the vital spark and energy, and some equate it with the soul.

The theory lost its prestige when organisms began to be seen as mechanisms with chemical and physical phenomena. However, as the limitations inherent in modern Western medical science—whose approach is based on mechanism theory, which treats the human body as a compound of individual parts—are revealed, alternative homeopathic therapies, including medical herbal therapy and Ayurveda, are being reevaluated.

Integrated medicine is the concept of combining conventional Western medical science and homeopathic therapies to achieve whole-person health. Often with a holistic approach, each person is treated as a whole person not only physically, but mentally, emotionally, and spiritually.

The word holistic is the adjective of holism, which means dealing with the whole of something. It comes from the Greek word *holos*. Whole, heal, holy, and health are all derivations of *holos*. As the early twentieth-century philosopher Jan Smuts said, "Even if you add up every single part, you can never reach the whole, because the whole is far greater than the collection of parts."

I have heard from several friends who have had disorders that they overcame them using a holistic approach, including dance therapy, counseling, or medicinal herb therapy. We are identifying increasing numbers of illnesses that cannot be well treated by Western science, and they are often related to stress and neurological imbalance. Since the 1950s, there have been more and more issues that cannot be treated and cured by Western medical treatments. Many alternative approaches that treat the body and mind as a whole—with no side effects—have been reevaluated. One plus one does not have to equal two; it can be three, four, or more, which is the effect known as synergy. We are the whole, and we are far greater than the collection of each organ and each part of our body.

DOLPHIN'S BLESSING

It was the last day of my stay at Izumo, Japan—often called the Land of God. I went to the tip of the peninsula to visit a museum and a shrine. The museum was built to exhibit a meteorite that had fallen on a resident's house some decades ago. My friends took me there to see the mysterious stone from the universe.

On the previous day, I was taken to a site deep in the mountain where there was a forest, which was discovered in the 1980s while they were developing the area and found the top of a cedar tree. Upon examination, it appeared to be a giant tree covered by volcanic ashes 4,000 years ago. They also found the remains of many other trees. The ancient forest was restored in a round modern building that showcases the mysterious forest using the latest technology. It has a spiral staircase along the wall around the trees. It was designed so visitors can walk down around the trees from the top to the bottom and see the forest from all angles.

In both the meteorite museum and the ancient forest site, I felt awe and wonderment like I was in a different space and time, light years away, 4,000 years earlier, and yet they were in front of my eyes enclosed in a modern building and coexisting with the latest technology.

Still unable to fully integrate what I saw and felt earlier, I was taken to Miho shrine, one of the oldest shrines in Japan, where the goddess of the sea is enshrined. Few people were in the shrine, and it was a perfect setting to quietly walk around and appreciate the mountain behind the shrine and the deep forest around it. I bowed and prayed for freedom and peaceful endeavors in the voyage of my life.

After we visited the shrine, we drove to the airport so I could catch my flight back to my hometown. On the road along the bay, I was sitting in the backseat of my friend's car and looking at the sea. My friend said people had recently spotted a mother and baby dolphin in the bay. I have seen and even swam with dolphins in Hawaii, but I never thought there were dolphins in the Sea of Japan, so I was looking at the sea while thinking, *Really? How could there be dolphins here?* The very next moment, a dolphin appeared and jumped above the surface of the water. The scene lasted only a few seconds, and I was the only person in the car who witnessed it.

I took the dolphin's jump as a sign of blessings. In some cultures, the dolphin is believed to be a messenger of balance, harmony, joyfulness, and playfulness. It was a perfect message for the final day of my trip. I was reassured that all I need to do is to be in balance with nature, the surrounding spirits, and my own spirit, and to remain joyful and playful.

A TASTE OF WATER IN AN EGYPTIAN VILLAGE

Have you ever experienced certain foods or drinks tasting different depending on the situation or your physical and psychological condition? Have you felt watermelon at the beach tastes sweeter, potato salad on a picnic table tastes better, or a glass of red wine smells more fragrant when you are in Europe?

One evening in a village along the tributary of the River Nile in Egypt, I went with a group of friends to visit a local family who invited us to dinner. The husband greeted us at the door and led us to their living/dining room to sit on a rug in a circle with the family. The food was laid out in front of us: home-baked bread, roasted fish, baked sweet potato, tahini, tajin, cucumber salad, tomato salad, spicy eggplant, leafy green sesame soup, and rice cooked with a local spice, all of which were prepared by the wife and served by the husband. Their children were shy at first, but soon curiosity overcame their shyness and they came to talk to us using the few English words they knew and with bright smiles.

The family does not drink alcohol. Instead, we were served water in a ceramic bottle we passed around the circle. I noticed the water was different as soon as I had my first sip. They did not have enough refrigeration, so it was not chilled, but the ceramic bottle kept the well water cool enough, and somehow, the water was so easy and mild to drink, as if it spread to each cell of my body once I drank it.

I can only guess, but it probably tasted different because the well water in the rural village was not polluted, had no chlorine added, and the River Nile and its soil contain rich minerals. The water in the ceramic bottle that was served by the host of the family was filled with hospitality, pure sincerity, and the family's kindness. I sensed all of them through my taste buds, including the smells in the air in the village, a little hazy purplish orange air at dusk, the touch of their daughter's little hands, and the family's laughter during the meal. These essences were all transferred into the water in the ceramic bottle.

I was grateful to be nurtured by the hearty meal, especially the water.

This experience showed me how obviously we are part of every other thing around us, living and non-living. It reminded me not to forget or neglect my physical and mental health and to use my five senses to feel different atmospheres and entities so I can fully appreciate and nurture my whole being.

AWAKENING IN SYNESTHETIC SENSES

Synesthesia is when one sense comes through as another. If you have synesthetic ability, you may define certain sounds as colors. For example, when you hear the "i" sound, you may see red and "a" as black.

There are many articles about synesthesia and famous people who are known to have this ability, including the composer Franz List, the jazz legend Duke Ellington, and the artist Vincent van Gogh.

Botanist, zoologist, biologist, anthropologist, ethologist, and author Lyall Watson, PhD, published *Gifts of Unknown Things* in 1976. It is a non-fiction work about his encounter with people on the extraordinary island of Nus Tarian, in Indonesia. Everyone on this island has synesthetic ability, some with stronger senses than others.

In conversation with a girl with an extra-strong synesthetic sense, he was fascinated by her ability. But for her it was natural, and she gave him a look of pity, knowing he didn't understand this simple concept.

She said:

How can you listen to other people and music if you do not see colors in them? When a drum talks, it spreads brown carpet that is as soft as the sand on the ground, and dancers stand on it. When a gong calls for green and yellow, we move around to make a pathway in the forest. Even if we are lost in the forest, a white string of the sound of flute shows us a way to come back home.

People on this island had integrated visual and audio senses so everyday reality contained miraculous phenomena, extrasensory perception, and psychic healing. And they see this sense as commonplace.

Watson's journey makes me wonder why we believe what we believe about reality. Perhaps, before humans started to use language, we lived in a world where the natural and the supernatural coexisted. Everyone had synesthetic ability and used it to live in harmony with other beings.

How rich could your world be if you saw colors and shapes in the sounds in your life? Perhaps we can use other senses, including touch and smell, in synesthetic ways if we remember the ability in our DNA and use it to live better and healthier lives. By wishing to cultivate and reawaken the ability, I make an effort to pull myself out of day-to-day mundane things and put myself in an environment where I can tone down my sympathetic nerve and make my parasympathetic nerve dominant.

Here is the list of things I do to nurture myself in a synesthetic way. I believe you, too, can nurture yourself by being more closely in touch with your senses and opening yourself up to your new world, which you never knew existed.

Making your daily routine a ritual: From the moment you wake up, you can make your day a ritual. When you make coffee, pay attention to the sound of water dripping from the bottom of the cone and inhale the fragrance of bittersweet beans. On your way to work, look around to see what color flowers are blooming in someone's front yard. When you feel the gentle breeze outside, imagine what color the wind might be.

Keeping your surroundings as comfortable as possible: You are absorbing everything, not only what you can see, hear, smell, touch, and taste, but also others' feelings, including people and other living beings. Be nice to others, including your family, friends, coworkers, and neighbors. And also be kind to animals and the planet itself. This will support health and happiness.

Eating healthily: You are what you eat. I support a plant-based diet, especially because eating lively plants grown in healthy soil gives you so much energy. I do not discourage fun dining at all. Moreover, I think people should enjoy eating more as a whole experience that includes ingredients, preparation, companions, and setting. It comes down to how much gratitude and appreciation you have and share with others.

1. **Being firm and defending yourself when you need to:** It is important to be grounded, especially when you explore new worlds by cultivating sensitivity. Your strength should be enhanced as you become sensitive, which you can do by feeling the "I" presence

around your hara, the center of your belly. Feel the warmth that is your source of energy and is always available when you need to access it. Your job is to keep your inner warmth. Be mindful to avoid being deceived by negative influences that wear you down and take your warmth away.

2. **Being open to wisdom:** What I am most grateful for is my experiences and the people I encountered through them. They are all my teachers. Some I made fond memories with, and others gave me a hard and challenging time. No matter what and how, they taught me important lessons integral to my growth. That became my wisdom, and no one can take it away. If you are having a hard time now, do not worry too much. It is normal to struggle sometimes. Just remember to appreciate and enjoy the process of becoming wiser.

EXERCISE

1. Write down the name of a person who gave you a hard time in the past. What did you experience through this person, and how did the experience influence you?

____

____

____

____

____

2. As you recalled memories of the person in exercise one, what color came to your mind? If you remember certain scenes, expressions, sounds, or tactile sensations, but you are not particularly comfortable with them, it may help you to recall them in colors. Once you assign the memories associated with that person a particular color in your imagination, blow that color away. Repeat this exercise and write down how the color changes every time you blow it away.

____

____

____

____

____

3. What would your life be like if you had not met the person you wrote about above? What wisdom did you gain from meeting them?

____

____

____

____

____

4. Write down the name of someone you have fond memories of. Assign the memories a color and blow the color away just as you did in exercise two. Blow it away whether bad or good so that you have no emotional attachment to it whatsoever. You do not need to worry about blowing the color away because your past remains within you. Instead, you are renewing and refreshing the color to ensure the flow of energy. Write down why you are grateful for that person after you blow the color away.

____

____

____

____

5. Rest and rejuvenate after you finish the exercises above. Those are energy works, and it is important to be aware of how energetically different you are after you have done the exercise and be kind to yourself. Have a cup of herbal tea with a spoonful of high-quality honey, take a warm bath, and/or smell your favorite essential oil. Write down how you feel.

____

____

____

____

SUMMARY

We are coexisting with other entities, including people, animals, insects, plants, stones, and all other elements in nature where billions of microorganisms reside. Your body is a miracle made of each organ, fluids, and cells, carrying bacteria that helps your body function well. Your nerves and sensors are directing you. By treating yourself as a whole and as if you are a super-sensitive, mysterious, and yet extraordinarily powerful being that can make miracles, you live to your full potential and can spread positive vibrations around, not only to yourself but to other people, to society, your country, the planet, future generations, and the whole universe. I hope you know now how important you are and you start treating yourself with full respect, hope, and love for your abilities.

Chapter 13

Surviving in Times of Chaos

"Through every kind of disaster and setback
and catastrophe, we are survivors.
And we teach our kids about that."

— Robert Fulghum

On August 8, 2023, I received a message from my friend on Maui telling me there was a huge fire in Lahaina and upcountry Maui. People on Front Street in Lahaina were jumping into the sea to escape the fire. I was vacationing in Japan at the time, and as soon as I realized it was not an ordinary brush fire, my heart started pounding. I called Kei immediately. He was staying in my house with my cat and confirmed he was safe—the fire didn't reach our area. I was relieved to know he was safe; however, being unable to calm my mind, I cancelled my plans and headed to the foot of the mountain where there was a shrine to the deity of rain. I wanted to pray. All I could do was to pray, and I am a believer in the power of prayer.

As I mentioned in the last chapter, when you see and treat yourself as a whole, you understand how beautiful and bright your core is. You see your inner strength and spiritual power. That is the power of humans, and all you need to do to access and use the power is believe in it.

What did I learn from the fire that destroyed Lahaina and took a hundred innocent lives? How are we going to recover from the loss, and how long will it take? What can I do for the community? How am I going to cope with the pain myself?

Writing is a powerful way of seeing and analyzing what is going on within the visible plain and being in touch with yourself and other spirits at a deeper level. I dedicate this chapter to the Maui fire and pray for Maui.

ISLAND OF ALOHA

If you have ever been to Maui, you know how special the island is. It is covered with lush green and colorful tropical flowers, surrounded by blue ocean and sky, birds are singing along with hula songs, and the trade wind is gently soothing on your skin. You feel close to nature and get healing energy from it. It is definitely one of the most beautiful places on earth, and I always feel so fortunate to have the opportunity to live there.

From ancient times, Hawaiians have lived on Maui with great respect for each element in nature. People know we are coexisting with nature, and nature give us abundance from the land and water. Before the United States took over the islands, Hawaiian people lived in villages along the slope of the land, and they diverted water from streams to make taro patches. Taro is their main staple, and taro patches need cold moving water to thrive. The ditches ran from the top of the mountain to the seashore. Along with taro, villagers who lived on higher land, which they call *mauka*, caught mountain animals and gathered mountain vegetables. On the middle plain, *kula*, they cultivated the land to grow fruits and vegetables. On the lower land, *makai*, they made fishponds to catch fish. They shared what they caught and grew among the villagers, took care of their children together, and lived in harmony within the community. In short, they possessed the Aloha spirit. According to the Hawaii Law of The Aloha Spirit in Chapter 5 of *Hawai'i Revised Statutes*:

> "Aloha Spirit" is the coordination of mind and heart within each person. It brings each person to the self. Each person must think and emote good feelings to others. In the contemplation and presence of the life force, "Aloha" is more than a word of greeting or farewell or a salutation. Aloha means mutual regard and affection and extends warmth and caring with no obligation in return. Aloha is the essence of relationships in which each person is important to every other person for collective existence. Aloha means to hear what is not said, to see what cannot be seen, and know the unknowable.

Aloha is described as the innate sense to love unconditionally. It is a symbiotic relationship you have with everything in the universe and recognizing your exact space within it. It is a life force, a connection to nature, an expression of love, and the hope it extends to the whole world.

Author and researcher for Hawaiian culture Pali Jae Lee wrote: "During ancient times, the only 'religion' was one of family and oneness with all things. The people were in tune with nature, plants, trees, animals, land, and each other. They respected all things and took care of all things."

I realized this Hawaiian thought of oneness with all things is very similar to Japanese thought from ancient times. You may be familiar with these thoughts called animism. In their 1990 book *A Hawaiian Nation: Man, Gods and Nature*, Michael Kioni Dudley and Keoni Kealoha Agard describe the early Hawaiian religion of animism this way:

> In the dominant current of Western thought there is a fundamental separation between humanity and divinity. In many other cultures, however, such differences between human and divine do not exist. Some peoples have no concept of a 'Supreme Being' or 'Creator God' who is by nature 'other than' creation.

Differences between human and divine and separation between humanity and divinity are concepts in monotheism, which is the belief that there is only one deity, a supreme being, also known as God. Monotheistic religions include the Abrahamic religions—Judaism, Christianity, and Islam—along with Zoroastrianism, Sikhism, etc.

LOOKING AT HISTORY

Hawaiian History

I believe it is important for us to understand history because behind the common image of Hawaii, the tropical paradise where life seems so easy and relaxed, many incidents and tragic conflicts took place that are not so well known. By putting a spotlight on these facts, we can help Maui to recover from its current situation, in which more than 6,500 people still do not have places to live after their houses were burnt in the August 8, 2023 Lahaina fire. It will also prevent us from letting similar things occur, such as despoliation of the lands, water, and people in the future. I've compiled the following history of Hawaii from numerous sources to give you an overview of why this history is important.[2]

Hawaii was an independent kingdom until 1893, when American and European capitalists and landholders overthrew the monarchy. The Hawaiian Islands, located in the center of the Pacific, provided a strategic location for a US military base and would help establish the US as a world superpower.

Prior to annexation by the United States, the Reciprocity Treaty of 1875 allowed sugarcane and other goods to be sold without tariff in the US. The treaty made Hawaii economically dependent on the US. The treaty led to the Bayonet Constitution in 1887, which King Kalakaua was

---

2 Among the key sources I used in creating this summary of Hawaiian history are *Women's Exchanges: The Sex Trade and Cloth in Early Nineteenth-Century Hawai'i*, a thesis written at the University of Hawaii, and the article "Captive Women in Paradise 1796-1826: The Kapu on Prostitution in Hawaiian Historical Legal Context" by Noelani Arista.

forced to sign at gunpoint. The constitution undermined the authority of King Kalakaua, took away Native Hawaiian land rights, and gave foreign landowners the vote.

Estimates show the death rate among Native Hawaiians accelerated devastatingly fast after first contact with Westerners. Captain Cook and his crew first arrived on the island of Kauai in 1778. Cook and his crew were welcomed by the Hawaiians, who were fascinated by the Europeans' ships and use of iron. Cook provisioned his ships by trading metal, and his sailors traded iron nails for sex. Cook and his crew wrote accounts about their concerns that they had infected the population with venereal diseases.

Over the years, many other diseases and illnesses such as measles, chicken pox, polio, and tuberculosis killed hundreds of thousands of Hawaiians. It is estimated one in seventeen Native Hawaiians died within two years of Cook's arrival.[3] By 1800, the population had declined by 48 percent. By 1820, it had declined 71 percent, and by 1840, it had declined 84 percent.

In 1820, the first New Bedford whaling ship hunted sperm whales on the "Japan Grounds" located halfway between Hawaii and Japan. The Hawaiian Islands became a perfect waypoint for stocking up on fresh local produce and water, making repairs, and finding new crew members.

---

3 See David Swanson. "A New Estimate of the Hawaiian Population for 1778, the Year of First European Contact." https://kamehamehapublishing.org/wp-content/uploads/sites/38/2020/09/Hulili_Vol11.2_Swanson.pdf. Accessed November 21, 2023.

Honolulu and Lahaina became the main Pacific ports for the North Pacific whaling fleet. Although Lahaina did not have a well-protected harbor like Honolulu, Lahaina Roads, the channel to the town of Lahaina, had a good anchorage for ships.

In 1824, more than 100 whaling ships anchored off Lahaina, and thirty years later, the number rose to 400 ships per year. Brothels, taverns, and inns sprung up along Front Street in Lahaina. Lahaina was not only the nexus of whaling prosperity but also of the Christian missionaries' influence.

The first Christian missionaries from the US mainland reached Hawaii in 1820. They settled first in Oahu, then quickly moved on to the neighboring islands. By 1835, many of Hawaii's chiefs had converted to Christianity, instructing their people to follow their lead.

The missionaries quickly established schools throughout the Islands, providing the Native Hawaiians with a written language, printed books, and training in the skills and trades suited to Western culture. Their influence on Hawaiian culture, family systems, the idea of land, monetary acquisition, and pleasure were beyond religion.

Prostitution was prohibited by Hawaiian chiefs in the 1820s; however, Hawaii was a contested site by trade, religious, and political interests. Euro-American sexual desires initiated a sex-for-goods trade in Hawaii. Prior to the coming of Western influence, the society recognized polyamorous unions and property was communal, so prostitution would have been a strange idea.

The first written record of a child traded for money in Hawaii comes from the diary of missionary Elisha Loomis. An American sea captain bought an eight-year-old, part-Hawaiian girl from her English sailor father in 1825. Her father ended up living in Hawaii and having multiple children with a local woman. This sailor had already sold his other daughters.

This little girl, Polly Holmes, escaped the American sea captain her father had sold her to and ran to the home of the high chief, Kalaimoku. Kalaimoku was horrified to learn about this incident and similar practices going on in the community.

The American sea captain demanded the child be returned. Kalaimoku refused and brought the girl into his court, thereby giving her protection. In his letters, Kalaimoku explicitly said it was against the traditions and customs of the land for anyone to be forced into sex or to be sold.

The slave-trading and prostitution of young girls became such a big concern because Hawaiian chiefs saw it as undermining Hawaiian society and it brought diseases. Thus the *kapu*, the prohibition of all forms of prostitution, was placed in 1825.

American missionaries supported the *kapu* due to their understanding of Christianity.[4] Between 1825 and 1827, the crews of two English whaling ships and an American warship rioted against these laws three times when they were unable to obtain Hawaiian women for sex.

---

4 See Adam Keawe Manalo-Camp, "The History of Human Trafficking in Hawaii." https://www.civilbeat.org/2018/10/the-history-of-human-trafficking-in-hawaii/. Accessed November 21, 2023.

During these armed attacks, mission stations in Honolulu and Lahaina were looted.

Hawaiian leaders resisted the sex trade at first. However, due to the rioting and foreign pressures, including naval power, the Hawaiian government became lax in enforcing prostitution laws. From letters between the island governors and the central royal government, we learn brothels began to operate in 1831 in Oahu and elsewhere.

Seeing no other options and with the decimation of the Native Hawaiian population, the Hawaiian government decided to allow a red-light district in the 1860s as a way to enforce health standards and minimize the abuses Native Hawaiian women faced.

Today, 160 years later, according to the US Census Bureau, if you look at the racial diversity in Hawaii, Asians, including Filipino, Japanese, Chinese, Thai, and Koreans, whose ancestors once worked in the Islands' sugarcane and pineapple fields are the largest ethnic group at 37 percent. Whites alone are 23 percent, and Native Hawaiians are only 10 percent.[5]

Meanwhile in Japan

Japan was closed to the West for two-and-a-half centuries until Commodore Matthew Calbraith Perry from the United States arrived and the long-secluded country opened its doors in 1853. Tokugawa shogunate, the military government of Japan at the time, upheld the

5 https://www.census.gov/quickfacts/fact/table/HI/PST045222. Accessed November 21, 2023.

isolation policy from concerns that outside influences would harm Japan, and the shoguns who ruled the country blocked foreigners from entering, even persecuting Christian missionaries who did enter the country.

Commodore Perry had gained fame as a hero in the Mexican-American War in 1848. The victory over Mexico not only added California to the United States, but opened a vista of new frontiers farther west across the Pacific Ocean. Japan, the land once called "Zipangu, the Land of Gold" by thirteenth-century Italian explorer Marco Polo, was an island nation surrounded by rich sea resources and full of people with "heathen souls," so it seemed to have infinite potential for the economic market and political as well as Christian influence.

After Japan was opened to the West, the Tokugawa shogunate, ended. With the new Meiji government, Japan started its industrial revolution, focused on economic growth, and adapted Western medicine and culture. It soon went to war with China and Russia, and then participated in the two world wars.

The Undersea Cable

According to Wikipedia, a submarine communications cable is a cable laid on the seabed between land-based stations to carry telecommunication signals across stretches of ocean and sea. The first submarine communications cables laid, beginning in the 1850s, carried telegraphy traffic, establishing the first instant telecommunications links between continents, such as the first transatlantic telegraph cable, which became operational on August 16, 1858. Submarine cables connecting all the world's continents, except Antarctica, were first laid in 1872, and subsequent generations of cables have carried telephone traffic, then data communications traffic to this day.

Constructing a submarine cable across the Pacific Ocean became a priority for the Western powers, especially the United States and the United Kingdom, in pursuit of their commercial and political interests in the Asian market and in their quest for empire.

According to the Japan Institute of International Affairs, the submarine cable's construction made a huge difference in Japan. While the new technology helped to modernize Japan's military and develop its national economy through the active participation of the newly emerged business community, the government was unable to formulate its own independent telecommunications policy due to control of the technology by foreign powers and corporations.

The construction of the Pacific Submarine Cable, designed to connect the North American and Asian continents, was regarded by both the US and the UK as an essential tool for penetrating the Asian market, especially the Chinese market. The two powers, therefore, considered Japan strategically important to their plan, thus drawing Japan into the politics of the Pacific Submarine Cable's construction.

In 1881, six years prior to his forced signing of the Bayonet Constitution, King Kalakaua of the Hawaiian Kingdom took a world tour. The tour was known as his attempt to save the Hawaiian culture and population from extinction by importing a labor force from Asia-Pacific nations. His first stop was Japan. Concerned over a possible United States seizure of the Hawaiian Islands, King Kalākaua had three proposals for the Emperor of Japan: 1) emigrating labor from Japan to Hawaii, 2) uniting the two nations with an arranged marriage between his five-year-old niece and the emperor's thirteen-year-old son, and 3) creating a union and federation of the Asiatic nations and sovereigns with Japan at its head. Within the third, he suggested installing a submarine cable between Hawaii and Japan.

The emperor only accepted the first proposal. Japanese immigrants working in plantation fields in Hawaii became the origin of today's majority Japanese population and their development of modern-day Hawaii. The second and the third proposals were declined for various reasons we can only imagine because history has always been written by the rulers.

LEARNING FROM HISTORY

As we look back on the events described above and the economic and political situations in Hawaii and Japan 150 years ago, I cannot stop thinking, *What if?*

What if these two nations had remained closed and maintained their own values, culture, and beliefs under their chiefs and shogun? What if they had been more knowledgably defensive on their own? What if they had realized how special their way of life was—so closely in harmony with other people and nature, without ego and attachment to materials and shallow human desire?

King Kalakaua was particularly fond of Japan because he felt some similarity between his people and the Japanese people. Perhaps that was because of Japanese spirituality, where we see spirits in nature and honor our ancestors and our lands, value family and people, and care for each other with love and compassion rather than control and enforcement.

THE POWER OF NATURE AND GOD/GODDESS

Many people still refer to God as he; however, the truth is God is neither a he nor a she because God is actually pure unconditional love and, hence, gender natural. Just for fun and balance, I often refer to God as she to make people think more deeply about the subject.

A little over a month after the Maui fire, two nights prior to the new moon, along with several women, I decided to go up to the 10,000-foot summit of Mount Haleakala. Haleakala means house of the sun in Hawaiian, and it is often referred to as the heart chakra of the earth.

Maui has a great community. People always help each other, and we have a strong sisterhood among friends in helping each other. We have been supporting each other through hardships, including the pandemic, for a long time; however, this time we were all devastated and experiencing tremendous grief.

This was not a normal wildfire. We all know that now. We know the lost lives and homes will not be back. We still do not know the real number of casualties, how long it will take to heal, or what future awaits for us here on the island.

We felt an urge to get closer to the sky, the universe, and also to the core of the earth, and the bottom of the sea, where some say ancient Lemuria exists in a different dimension. We can remember we all came from the universe and are made out of stardust there.

I wanted to tune into dolphins and whales and their vibration, which is as delightful as the laughter of little children. I needed to embrace their existence with warmth in my heart, which felt bleeding red blood from being stabbed by knives of sorrow, and I wanted to transform and transcend my heart's pain with the blue flame of a healing vibration.

We reached the summit above the cloud as the sun was getting closer to the horizon. The sky was glowing pink, orange, and green. We sat quietly, licked some sacred sea salt to purify ourselves, and started to pray while gazing at every precious moment of the sunset. A Hawaiian chant was recited, and everyone at the summit listened humbly to the sincere prayer, asking for guidance from above.

I had come up to the summit many times before, and every time I was at this spot, I was struck by this magnificent mountain and the sky. This time, I was preparing to give prayers for healing—healing of people in Lahaina, Maui, and also for myself—and I also wanted to ask for guidance from the Universe, Source, God, or whatever you name it. However, for half an hour or so, while I was watching the sunset and the ever-changing hues of the sky, all I had in my mind was gratitude. If I could describe my heart in words at that time, I would only say thank you.

Not a single moment is the same. Each will never come back again once it passes. All the pain and sorrow are things of the past, as the joy and beauty in the moment are never going to be repeated.

It is up to you whether you seek joyous and beautiful feelings or stay in sadness and misery every precious moment.

What I learned through the Maui fire was all cultures have a dark history no one is proud of, and the blame can be placed on the dark energies of any era anywhere on earth in history. However, just because this dark energy persists and some of its evil has perpetuated the kingdom of Hawaii, the country of Japan, and many other civilizations throughout time and the world, it does not mean we can forget the goodness of humans and give up our will and kind nature—our ability to show compassion and empathy to each other.

I also learned during this time of disaster in Maui that it is completely normal to feel the emotions of sadness, grief, pain, and anger; however, to heal as a community, as an island, as a culture, we have to turn this disaster over to the Divine and ask him/her to transmute these challenging emotions into love. When you do that, it removes the burden, pain, and emotions from your shoulders. Sincerely ask God/ Goddess, Universe, ancestors, Divine Mother, or whatever you name the Divine to take over your pain and grief. This ultimately frees your emotions to be in a state of empathy, compassion, and unconditional love.

TRANSFORM PAIN INTO UNCONDITIONAL LOVE

I want to share five strategies for when you experience disaster. It can be a natural disaster or any disastrous situation.

1. **Go to the most beautiful place you can think of and be grateful:** I feel fortunate to live on the island of Maui where you can access nature so easily. Wherever you live, go find the most serene spot you can. It can be under a certain tree, along a little stream, or in the middle of a flower garden. If you live in a concrete jungle and you have a hectic lifestyle, just look up at the sky at least once a day, but as many times as possible. Take a quiet moment, put your hands on your heart, and ask yourself, "How are you?" Feel the warmth of your own heart and wait for the feeling of gratitude to come out. You must be grateful for your heartbeat, and once you are in touch with the feeling of gratitude, it will spread all around you.

2. **Remember that all things change:** Regardless of how much pain you are carrying or how much fun you are having, the situation will change. From ancient times, Egyptians used blue lotus flowers for various rituals. The lotus flower blooms above the surface of muddy water, closes at night, and reopens in the morning. It is believed that every night, the flower becomes a bed for the sun god Ra. It embraces him by its thousand petals for him to rest and to rejuvenate, and it reopens the next morning when he goes out into

the world to brighten it with his renewed power. When you go to bed tonight, imagine you are embraced by soft and delicate petals, and you are safely protected in the fragrant flower that gives you rejuvenation and relaxation. You will wake up as a new goddess/god the next morning filled with energy and power.

3. **When you focus on love, you keep dark energy at bay:** The key to focusing on love is to always remember the most important thing in your life. When you encounter disaster and are in a challenging situation, it might be hard to believe everything happens for a reason, and the reason is for love. What the Universe wants you to learn is to love yourself so you become stronger, believe in yourself, remember your inner power to live your life fully, and remember your mission and your goal is to live your life as a human on the planet earth.

4. **Accept some things are beyond your control:** The earlier you accept that you can't control everything, the sooner you can be free from burden. When you face disasters such as war, fire, illness, or separation, you may be caught in a heavy feeling of guilt and self-blame. You might wonder if you could have prevented it, or if you could have taken different actions. Once you start thinking that way, you can be caught in an endless loop of regret and anger for a long time. It is important to live now, not in the past. Remind yourself it is not your fault, and it is not your responsibility to take care of everything that happens around you, so you should stop blaming yourself. You have so much to do in this lifetime, and you can do those things better by being free from negative emotions and being lighthearted, so it is very important to let go.

5. **Learn history and focus on the good:** To prevent the dark energy of the past from recurring, it is important to learn the history of your culture and focus on the good instead of the bad. Have you ever heard stories from your family or elders about what their lives were like during World War II, the Korean War, or the Vietnam War, and wondered how such devastatingly cruel wars could ever happen? How can we allow ourselves to kill millions of innocent civilians? Have you then given further thought about why we still have wars? Haven't we learned anything from history?

    If you ever wonder about the mysteries behind disasters, including wars, dig deeper and research for yourself to see the facts with your own eyes instead of blindly believing what you've been told. You may encounter unbelievable stories and facts that have been hidden or distorted. They can be somewhat shocking and uncomfortable at first, but I believe it is our responsibility to pass down true history to future generations.

    Let's shine a light on the mistakes and failures of our past so our children can learn from them, become wiser than we are, and make the world a better place. If we keep on ignoring history and how we caused disasters, the mistakes will most likely recur. We should learn from the mistakes our ancestors made and become better humans. I believe that is what our ancestors are wishing for us.

    Our ancestors are watching with their loving souls, and you should be proud of yourself for being courageous, keeping your eyes wide open, and taking every step out of your way for your children and your loved ones. No matter what culture you are from, whatever the history, there have always been loving and caring heroines/heroes like you in past, and that is why you and I exist now, breathing every day, enjoying the breeze and fragrance of flowers, and listening to the laughter of children.

Let's not forget our ancestors' love; let's pass down their legacy; and let's work to grow their love into the next level, unconditional love, which is for our children and generations to come.

EXERCISE

1. What disaster have you experienced? It may be an earthquake, fire, flood, disease, conflict, or anything else that had shocking and devastating effects.

____

____

____

____

____

____

2.   How did you go through that disastrous experience physically and
     emotionally?

     ____

     ____

     ____

     ____

     ____

3.   How did a God, Goddess, the Universe, Source, or whatever you
     call it play a role in helping you in the hard time?

     ____

     ____

     ____

     ____

     ____

4.   What is your pain level on a scale of one to ten when you close your
     eyes, think of that hard time, put your hands on your heart, and feel it?

     ____

     ____

     ____

5. How many years or days have passed since you experienced the disaster? You may be amazed to see how long the pain can last in your heart. If you want the pain to be gone, verbally ask a Goddess, God, the Universe, or Source to take it away, or rather ask them to let you release your pain for them to handle. They will gladly take it and make it into love and return it to the earth. You may want to do so in a quiet, peaceful environment. After doing so, measure your pain level again and write it down below.

____

____

____

____

SUMMARY

Aloha means to hear what is not said, to see what cannot be seen, and to know the unknowable. When you experience disaster, it can be hard to overcome the pain, grief, and anger. However, if you focus on the unconditional love you receive from your ancestors and great spirits around you or from the Universe, you realize the importance of passing down love to your children and future generations. We are living in a crucial era when revolution is happening, and all of us are involved in making the greatest revolution of love on this planet, Earth.

Chapter 14

Returning to Your Soul's Home

"We are just walking each other home."

— Ram Dass

Being from Japan, the concept of reincarnation is natural to me. Our souls are all going to heaven when we die and leave our physical form. Then we are going to begin a new life in another body. We are in the infinite cycle of life that is the universal law. What I have learned living in America is that most Americans are afraid of death—so much so that people do not believe life continues after death and our souls go to heaven to be prepared to be reborn into the next life.

Knowing the concept of reincarnation can be your pivotal point. You come from heaven, and you go home to heaven. As I wrote in the last chapter, when you experience chaos and disaster, the more pain you feel, the harder it may be for you to let go. That is because the pain you are carrying might not be only yours but the accumulation of pain from previous generations. One of the most important assignments you have in this lifetime is to let go of all the pain of your ancestors, including that of your father and mother, grandparents, and great-grandparents, and also your pain from past lives. Let go of all the pain experienced and the pain that you and they did not, or rather could not, let go of and transform it into love. Your soul is carrying all those memories, and even though your conscious mind does not remember, you feel it in your heart.

We have talked about how you handle the pain in your heart when you are in disastrous situations and how it is so important to turn your sadness and anger over to a God/Goddess, the Universe, your ancestors, or some greater power than yourself. Once you release your negative emotions, your Higher Power takes them over and will gladly transform them into unconditional love, then pour that love over us on earth like blessed rain. At the same time, you will be given your ancestors' guidance, the guidance to live as who you are, and that is what matters.

In this chapter, let's talk about your journey to your soul's home. Home can be the town where you grew up that holds your childhood memories or heaven where you go after you leave your physical form. Going home is the moment of being reborn and starting afresh—being lighthearted as you live your life as who you are and shine as brightly as a star in the sky. You coexist with billions of other stars and are embraced by the infinite Universe we all came from, which is unconditional love itself.

STARTING AFRESH ALL OVER AGAIN

One of my favorite quotes is by writer Doug Cooper: "It may not be the life you imagined, but it's your life. You came here for a reason. Is it time for you to go and begin again?"

We all came here for a reason. I think life is like a quest to find our own reason for coming to live in this lifetime, and on our quest, we have times when we must say goodbye to our past and hello to a new stage of our life that leads our soul closer to home, which is ultimately heaven.

When the Maui fire happened, in the midst of the shock and grief, I felt it was time to leave my beloved Maui and go back to my hometown in Japan. I felt I had things to do in my home country.

When I first heard about the massive fire in Maui while vacationing in Japan, I knew it was devastating, so I prayed. I prayed for rain, for the water of purification for humanity, and for peace to bring us together to raise our consciousness.

While I was praying, a jewel beetle flew by me. In our culture, jewel beetles are used in decorative boxes and even religious shrines. Throughout time, jewel beetles have been seen as symbols of good luck and protection from evil. When a beetle lands on you, they offer protection from bad energy and invite fortune into your life. I think part of the reason jewel beetles have such an auspicious reputation is because they are living fire detectors—the jewel beetle can sense forest fires from afar, moving in quickly to lay its eggs in the smoldering bark of burnt trees, where its young develop virtually free of competition.

This was my first encounter with a living jewel beetle, and I saw the beetle as a messenger of a greater being, like an angel. The jewel beetle flew to me to bring protection and good fortune, and at the same time it also brought me a message of warning as a living fire detector. The Maui fire was a tragic and unfortunate event. It was not just something tragic happening on a tropical island 4,000 miles away—it could come to the island nation of Japan too. By looking at history, I have learned that we, Hawaii and Japan, are especially connected.

It is time to change our history. Some say history repeats itself, but does it really have to? Isn't it time for us to change and begin again? I strongly feel it is our time to declare enough is enough and end our cycle of wars and conflicts on earth, which are caused by greed and cruelty— keeping humans in agony and despair. It is our time to unite and raise our vibrations to a height where evil energy cannot enter or give harm.

LISTENING TO YOUR SOUL AND GOING HOME

You may wonder how we can rise and, at the same time, be rooted unshakably? If you think it is too hard to shake off your doubt, fear, and feeling of powerlessness, I want you to know it is not yours. Self-doubt was given to you in your upbringing by your parents or some other adults who raised you. Your parents raised you to think you are powerless because they were raised that way by their parents. See the repeating pattern? Are you raising your children the same way, or are you teaching them they can be extraordinary?

I was repeating the pattern. Now my son is an adult in his late twenties. Instead of being constantly worried about him and giving him too much direction by trying to protect him with an imaginary safe bubble, I wish I had raised my son to believe he is a powerful being surrounded by and filled with love. The principle of the Universe is that no matter what they do, every person on the planet plays a central role, and I wish for him to know it.

If you are like me and wish for your children to live happily, you can show them how you are true to your heart and it is where your soul's home is.

As stated earlier, after the divorce, I took my son and moved to the Bay Area in California and started my new life in America. I got married for the second time, raised my new family, built my career in the food industry, and went through my spouse's illness and death in the ten years I lived in the Bay Area. After I moved to Maui eight years ago, I established my plant-based food business and ran an organic farm with accommodations for private retreats.

Maui was my dream home. Its beautiful nature and the wonderful friends I made on the island gave me so much healing and comfort, and I have learned so much through my experiences and interactions there. I thought it might be my last home because I love my life on Maui so much. However, the Universe had a different plan for me.

As I listen to my soul, I know the time has come. I am going home to the town where my elderly parents await. I go home for love—love for my family, for my beloved, and for my motherland. I am supported by unconditional love from the Universe, my ancestors, and Mother Earth.

I gladly follow where God leads. That is how I live as who I am, and I remain close to my home, which helps lead my soul to heaven.

Listen to your soul and feel how closely you are living to your true self. Are you following your dream? Is the dream from your heart?

BECOMING FRIENDS WITH YOUR HEART

In the international bestselling novel *The Alchemist* by Paulo Coelho, the main character, Santiago, is a young Andalusian shepherd who dreams of a treasure while in a ruined church. A fortune teller tells him treasure is in the Egyptian pyramids, so he sets out on a journey to find it. Along his journey, Santiago meets people, falls in love, and learns many things through his experiences. When he finally reaches the pyramid, he realizes the treasure he sought was where he had his original dream all along.

Santiago encounters a wise alchemist who teaches him to realize his true self. The alchemist says, "There is only one way to learn. It's through action. Everything you need to know you have learned through your journey."

The alchemist also says:

Before a dream is realized, the Soul of the World tests everything that was learned along the way. It does this not because it is evil, but so that we can, in addition to realizing our dreams, master the lessons we've learned as we've moved toward that dream. That's the point at which most people give up.

If you think about what the alchemist said, you realize all the lessons you have learned were provided so you could master them, and what's important is to keep trying and moving forward.

MASTERING THE LESSONS AND REALIZING YOUR DREAM

Life is like a journey seeking the treasure buried deep in your heart, and the treasure is your dream. All the challenges and hardships you experience teach you something, and you master them so you can keep getting closer to your true self. You bring the treasure you find in this lifetime, which is your dream, to heaven at the end of this lifetime, and the treasure you found will be shared in heaven with other souls who brought back treasure in their quest. The treasure will be greater if you master the lessons as you seek harder and dig deeper into your heart.

Stop being afraid of suffering. People have a hard time letting go of the fear of suffering because it is familiar. It is familiar because you grew up hearing how fearful the human history of suffering is, and you have been taught to believe in a life and future full of misery and hardship—in short, you learned humans are meant to suffer. This is a false belief that has been manipulating us for thousands of years. Suffering and struggle come into your life so you can conquer them and advance your quest to find your true self—life's obstacles are your adventure. So, rather than being afraid, feel free to take your adventure of life's ups and downs and enjoy lifelong excitement.

The truth is in your soul. If you go deeper into your heart and remember where you came from, your soul knows to flip suffering into love, which is actually very simple—you must believe in the presence of a God/Goddess, "the Soul of the World," and that we are all connected as family in the universe.

BELIEVING IN LOVE

Love is your soul's core—that is a simple fact. And yet, you are exposed to many distractions and may have a hard time remembering and believing in that love sometimes. I want to share these five strategies to help you stay centered in love—they are reminders for myself as well.

1. **Love is you, and you are love:** If you look at your soul, you can see how brightly it shines. You are a shining star—this is an absolute truth. Let's use your imagination and look at yourself from a bird's eye view when you were a newborn baby. See the happiness you radiate and give to your mother, father, and the other people around who are looking at the newborn you. You are the greatest miracle of hope as you enter this world. You still cannot even open your eyes and can barely move your tiny legs and arms; you are unable to support your own head, and you just sleep most of the time. A baby does nothing but simply exist, yet it is the most amazing gift to the world—and the baby is you. You, simply by existing, are a miracle, the miracle of love for a child.

2. **Your soul never dies—you came from heaven, and you will return to heaven:** You were born in this lifetime as a human being on the planet earth. You have a human form, a gender, a language, and people who interact and connect with you. This is your outer condition, which was what you chose prior to being born on planet earth. You have some purpose to pursue, to make some progress on to bring back home to heaven when you finish. Next time, you may or may not come back as a human on earth. You may not have a physical form, and you may not come to this planet, which means you may not have sight to look at the colors of the rainbow, scent to smell fragrant roses, hearing to listen to a bird's song, taste to enjoy the sweetness of a peach, touch to feel the warmth of the heart, and a brain to imagine a better world. So, why not appreciate and enjoy each precious moment of this lifetime by using what you have as a human on this beautiful planet?

3. **Know your purpose and never give up:** Your purpose on earth is to live as truly as who you are as you can and continuously seek what you want to be. It is your soul's infinite quest because the act of seeking itself is your assignment. And it is an act of love because love is passion's fuel, and without passion, you will not have energy to seek.

4. **You are contributing to the universe by simply believing in love and by loving others:** You, I, and all living beings originate from the Soul of the World that is the universe. According to some interpretations of the Akashic Records, eons ago there was harmony in the universe, but the galactic spirit thought harmony

was not enough to make the universe evolve—it needed love. Therefore, the spirit tasked a god and a goddess to make a new family meant to activate this universe by love.

Earth has a special mission to grow many kinds of living beings. That is why the earth was given an abundance of water. The earth started from inside, pushing out volcanic energy through magma, which was Terra. Gaia gave her water to Terra, and thus life was born and nurtured. That is our ancestor.

Billions of years later, we are alive on this planet, born of father and mother, who are children of Terra and Gaia, and our mission is to love, which is needed to activate and evolve our universe.

Remember, to love and be loved, teach our mission of love to your children—that is how all of us can thrive on Mother/Father Earth.

5. **Remember you are never alone:** You are always supported not only by your friends and family, who are in this dimension of the world, but also by your ancestors, spirits of nature, and angels. These are in different dimensions and, hence, invisible to your physical eyes; however, they are always available for you, and once you call to ask for their support, they are happy to help you. That is because they want you to believe in them and communicate with them. Believing and communicating are spontaneously initiated only by love. Love is mutual, and that is why your willingness is essential. They very much want to raise your vibration, which leads others to be raised through the contagious and transmuting effect of love.

EXERCISE

1. Have you thought about what happens to you after you die and leave your physical form? Whether you have or not, think about it and describe your thoughts below.

____

____

____

____

____

____

2. Put your hands on your heart, feel its beat and warmth, and ask yourself, "What is my dream?" If you cannot hear its answer, keep asking the same question every day for two weeks, and your heart will respond to your sincerity. Write down the answer below.

____

____

____

____

____

3. Once you know your dream, it is time to act. What action do you think you need to take to pursue your dream?

____

____

____

____

____

4. If you see obstacles or have doubts about your ability to take the action you described above, think about where these thoughts originated. Do they come from your soul or some other beings, including your inner child, parents, and ancestors?

____

____

____

____

____

5. If you see/have them, embrace the obstacles and self-doubt you were carrying as representative of your past. Do so for a moment in your heart while you are feeling the warmth of your own heart. Then let it go to the angels who are here to support you so you can remove

your burden and raise your vibration to pure love. Write down how you feel now, and if you got inspiration by communicating with angels, describe it below.

____

____

____

____

____

____

SUMMARY

Love yourself, believe in love, be in love, cherish love, and spread love—that is the most important thing you need to pursue in this lifetime because you are given your life as a human on earth, the planet in this galaxy, with the mission of love.

Every day, you are given opportunities to connect to your soul. Every morning, you have sunrise, which itself is an action and reminder of love. Cherish each moment, and the rest will be guided by the Soul of the World with much support from others, including your past self, your ancestors, and your angels, who are all your family.

Always Remember to Be Love

"People where you live grow five thousand
roses in one garden...
yet they don't find what they're looking for…
And yet what they're looking for could be
found in a single rose...
But eyes are blind.
You have to look with the heart."

— Antoine de Saint-Exupéry

Now that you have read my book, what actions are you going to take? I hope you now understand and are aware of the importance of practicing the art of love and trying most actively to live in the art of love.

Discipline is virtue, but I want to emphasize more specifically the importance of self-discipline in achieving the art of love because it is a more enjoyable form of practice than being obedient to some strict rules. You can transform the knowledge you received by reading this book into power by applying it in your everyday life. Think about all the cookbooks you may have seen in the past—if you don't try any of the recipes, you will never get to taste how delicious they are.

On the ten exercise lines below, list the ten actions you are committed to taking within the next ninety days as a result of reading this book.

Layout, stretch the lines below to the right margin

1. ____

2. ____

3. ____

4. ____

5. ____

6. ____

7. ____

8. ____

9. ____

10. ____

In this book, you learned how to clear the path on the art of love and maintain it so it gets easier to connect with your soul. Remember to treat your body as if God exists within, and offer your respect and gratitude. Observation is the first step to realization, and once you have realization, you can accelerate the process of getting in touch with your intuition. Your keen interest to go deeper and deeper inside yourself to find the truth about who you are and what you want to do is indeed an essential asset for your creativity.

We are creatures who live in community, which can come in any form, including family, neighbors, school, clubs, and so on, and we always feel secure and protected by the warmth of other people's hearts. By looking at the people who had the strongest influence on you, often your family, you find out what you learned from them from birth— and you realize you learned things even before you had a cognitive mind. By accessing both motherhood and fatherhood within yourself, which naturally invoke images of the positive aspects of feminine and masculine, you will have a better understanding of what divine feminine and divine masculine mean.

Having compassion for yourself is fundamentally important for healing yourself. Meditation is used to look inside of your soul, and when you sense your soul as a vibrant being, you can believe in your own beauty and strength, and you can know you are much more than what you possess or your outer look. You can attain love if you are determined and believe in yourself. Always listen to what your heart tells you first.

You put out your vibration of hope and belief, and you receive help and support from the Universe—you cannot know when and in what form, but you will be honored to receive it when it is given as your reward for loving yourself and loving life.

Life is like a journey seeking the treasure buried deep in your heart, and the treasure is your dream. All the challenges and hardships you experience during your lifetime help you learn, and each challenge you master brings you closer to your true self.

If you apply the wisdom, knowledge, experience, skills, strategies, and techniques offered in this book, you will achieve what the title and subtitle promise, which is *Embracing the Art of Love*, and *Healing Your Past, Regaining Your Power, Following Your Soul*!

I want to leave you with something I wrote many years ago that I shared at the beginning of this book:

> "Imagine a world where all mothers are smiling.
> Hold the warmth in your heart.
> See the light your soul radiates.
> You are the creation of love.
> Love is who you are."

I encourage you to contact me to tell me what you liked about my book and what you disliked so I can improve it for the next printing. More importantly, tell me about you, your challenges, and your obstacles and adversities so I can help you.

My email address is ayako@embracingtheartoflove.com, so please feel free to reach out to me with your thoughts, comments, and suggestions.

I wish you love!

Your friend,

Ayako Kondo

About the Author

AYAKO KONDO is an author, professional keynote speaker, life coach, and ambassador for divine feminine principles. She developed her beliefs in these areas over the years through encounters with different cultures and philosophies. She understands we are facing a crucial time of revolutionary change and feels what can help the world and the human race most is to follow the principle of love and forgiveness.

Ayako was born and raised in Japan. For the past thirty years, she has moved to various places including China, Taiwan, California, and Hawaii in search of her dreams, independence, and freedom. Ayako has studied and learned different languages, cultures, national histories, and philosophies. She has also participated in various spiritual practices, including Zen, Vipassana meditation, and reiki healing, and she has been trained in clairvoyant energy work. Ayako is certified in plant-based nutrition by T. Colin Campbell, and she has conducted cooking classes in Hawaii and Japan. She established an organic farm and accommodations, and also ran her own plant-based food company on Maui.

Now Ayako is transitioning from Maui to Japan to be close to her aging parents, and she also feels the need to spread the divine feminine principle to her native country. Ayako lives by following her dream and passion, which is to fill the world with children's laughter and the loving smiles of all people.

In her personal time, Ayako enjoys reading, learning about various topics, practicing medicinal herb therapy, going to museums and galleries, hiking in nature, walking on the beach, and gathering with friends. She loves flowers, beauty, and good food. Ayako absolutely adores her cat, Tane-chan, which is a Japanese word meaning "seed."

About the Cover

The painting on the front cover is by Kana Anan, an artist in residence in Maui, Hawaii. The scene depicted takes place at night. The lei is a garland, symbolizing love and friendship, of roses floating on water. Ayako wanted to put her wish for love to the world on the cover of her book, so she asked Kana to use Mother Mary blue in the background and a lei of lokelani rose. Lokelani is the flower of Maui, and the rose is the flower with the highest vibration and a symbol of the divine feminine. Ayako wanted to convey the message of love from the Divine Mother in the blue traditionally associated with Mother Mary and the beauty of friendship in the lei-connection of flowers. Kana was inspired by Ayako's intention and depicted it in her art as the lei floating on water. Ayako hopes the cover itself tells a story of love and that it sends a healing prayer for Maui and for all over the world.

About Ayako Kondo Coaching

*I*f you want to live in the art of love, the most important thing is to be gentle and tender with yourself. You need to develop the habit of checking in with your heart to see if it is filled with love and to care for yourself first before moving outward to help others.

The art of love is practiced by embracing every moment and everything around you. When you speak, you speak as if you embrace each word that comes out of your mouth.

Do you remember which foot you put on the floor first when you got out of bed this morning? When was the last time you looked at the orange and pink hue of the sky around sunset? Do you feel happy if someone greets you by saying, "Welcome home!" when you return home?

These feelings are all important to living in the moment and finding joy in every precious living moment. We all live in the busy modern world and are accustomed to thinking and acting efficiently. However, the most efficient way to live would be to seek death as soon as possible right after you were born.

Efficiency is not the way to live. Each action you take, every word you speak, how you think, and everything you encounter is there to help fulfill your heart through the love of living your life. Let's talk about the feelings in your heart more than what is happening around you!

Ayako Kondo's coaching focuses on listening to your heart, listening to yourself, and being your own best friend. These are the fundamental skills you will learn from her while learning to practice the art of love.

For more information, visit Ayako's website at the address below, or contact her through email to schedule a thirty-minute, complementary consultation via phone or video call.

www.EmbracingTheArtOfLove.com
Ayako@EmbracingTheArtOfLove.com

Book Ayako Kondo to Speak at Your Next Event

AYAKO KONDO is passionate about making others aware of the importance of the art of love, especially in a world where conflicts and struggles abound. So many people, including children, often have trouble with stress, depression, and anxiety. As the title of her book, *Embracing the Art of Love*, represents, she speaks as if she embraces each word that comes out of her mouth, which is how the divine feminine holds the event and audience.

Whether your audience is ten or ten thousand, at a corporate office or in a school, Ayako can deliver a divine masculine and/or divine feminine speech geared to your audience. Ayako understands your audience does not want to be taught anything, but is interested in hearing stories of inspiration, encouragement, different cultures, and philosophies that can change their lives.

If you are looking for a different, one-of-a-kind speaker who will leave your audience wanting more, book Ayako Kondo today!

To find out whether Ayako is available for your next meeting, visit her website at the address below. You can contact her through email as well to schedule a complementary, pre-speech phone interview.

www.EmbracingTheArtOfLove.com

Ayako@EmbracingTheArtOfLove.com